GCSE

Questions and Answers

ENGLISH

KEY STAGE 4

Ian Barr Chief Examiner
Chris Walton Examiner

Letts
EDUCATIONAL

SERIES EDITOR: BOB McDUELL

Letts Educational
Aldine Place
London W12 8AW
Tel: 0181 740 2266
Fax: 0181 743 8451
e-mail: mail@lettsed.co.uk
website: http://www.lettsed.co.uk

First published 1995
Reprinted 1995 (twice), 1996
Revised 1996, 1997

Text: © Ian Barr and Chris Walton 1995, 1996, 1997

Design and illustrations: © BPP (Letts Educational) Ltd 1995, 1996, 1997

British Library Cataloguing in Publication Data
A CIP record for this book is available from the British Library.

ISBN 1 85758 608 5

Acknowledgements
Every effort has been made to trace copyright holders and to obtain their permission for the use of copyright material. The authors and publishers will gladly receive any information enabling them to rectify any error or omission in subsequent editions.
　　All answers are provided by the author. Permission for reproduction of questions from past papers has been granted by – or is pending from – the examination boards listed below. None of the boards has provided answers and none accepts responsibility for the answers suggested by the author. Answers provided may not necessarily constitute the only possible solutions.
　　Task 3 (p63) and Task 8 (p71): Reproduced by the Midland Examining Group. Question on p17: Reproduced by kind permission of the University of Cambridge Local Examinations Syndicate. The Midland Examining Group and the University of Cambridge Local Examinations Syndicate bear no responsibility for the example answers to questions taken from their past question papers which are contained in this publication. Task 4 (p63): Reproduced by kind permission of the Northern Examinations and Assessment Board. The authors accept responsibility for answers provided, which may not necessarily constitute the only possible solutions. Task 6 (p66): Reproduced by kind permission of the Scottish Qualifications Authority (formerly SEB). Answers are the sole responsibility of the authors and have not been provided by the Board. Task 7 (p68): Reproduced by kind permission of London Examinations: A division of Edexcel Foundation (formerly ULEAC). Edexcel Foundation, London Examinations accepts no responsibility whatsoever for the accuracy or method of working in the answers given. Task 5 (p65): Reproduced by kind permission of the Welsh Joint Education Committee. Poems on p14 are reproduced from Poems from Seamus Heaney, published by Faber and Faber. Article on p18 reproduced with permission from the May 1995 *Reader's Digest* magazine. Copyright © Reader's Digest Association May 1997. Extract on p22 reproduced by arrangement with Watts Books, a division of the Watts Publishing Group, London, from *Life Guides: The Environment and Health* by Brian Ward. Extract on p16 reproduced from *Ice Trek* by Ewan Clarkson. Extract on pp24–5 reproduced from *Pole to Pole* by Michael Palin with the permission of BBC Enterprises Limited. Article on p38 reproduced with kind permission from an article by Brian Jenkins in *The Independent*, January 24 1994. Article on p43–5 reproduced from the *AA magazine*, Issue 13, Summer 1995. Photographs on p43–5 by Richard Newton. Illustration on p44 by Tim Slade. Poem on p56 reproduced from *Standing Female Nude* by Carol Ann Duffy, published in 1995 by Anvil Press Poetry Ltd. Extract on p57 reproduced from *American Short Stories of Today* published by Penguin, and originally in an anthology published by Faber and Faber. Article on pp59–61 adapted and reproduced from an article by Peter Silverton, © the Observer. Photograph on p62 by Nils Jorgensen © Rex Features Ltd. Photograph on p63 by Haywood Magee © Hulton Deutsch. Extract on pp64–5 adapted from *Some Day My Prince Will Come* by Deborah Moggach. Photograph on p66 reproduced by permission of BUPA. Extract on pp67–8 reproduced from *Flag on the Island* by V S Naipaul, published by André Deutsch.

Prepared by *specialist* publishing services, Milton Keynes

Printed in Great Britain by Ashford Colour Press

Letts Educational is the trading name of BPP (Letts Educational) Ltd

Contents

HOW TO USE THIS BOOK

Although this book has been fairly substantially revised for 1998, its aim remains to provide you, the student, with the help you need to reach the highest level of achievement possible in one of your most important examinations – the General Certificate of Secondary Education (GCSE) or, in Scotland, at General and Credit levels. The book is designed to help all students, up to and including A* grade at GCSE.

Undoubtedly you will know that syllabuses have been revised substantially for 1998 and the authors have checked changes in the style of questioning associated with the revised syllabuses. We continue in our belief that experienced Examiners can provide, through examination questions, sample answers and advice, the help a student needs to ensure success.

The primary consideration has been to present the main principles on which study can be based so that confidence can grow as weaknesses are identified and eliminated.

The *Questions and Answers* series is designed to provide:

- Easy-to-use **Revision summaries** which identify important information which the student must understand if progress is to be made answering examination questions. Spend some time on this section first and refer back to it whenever you find it necessary. There should not be anything in this section which is brand new; you will find that you have covered all the things referred to in class, but it will be useful to remind yourself of all the things covered in this section.

- Advice on the **different types of task** (or question) and how to answer them well to obtain the highest marks. We have included in the book a range of different types of task using **different types of stimulus material**. In one sense the technique you should use is always the same – read the stimulus material carefully, make notes, think and then complete the task taking care to revise your first attempt. However, associated with each task, or set of tasks, are specific notes which should help you both in approaching what you have to do and in reviewing what you have done.

- Information about other skills which will be tested on examination papers apart from the recall of knowledge. These are sometimes called **Assessment Objectives**. Modern GCSE examinations put great emphasis on the testing of objectives other than knowledge and understanding. Assessment objectives include communication, problem solving, evaluation and interpretation.

- The book contains many examples of **examination questions**. A student can improve by studying a sufficiently wide range of questions providing they are shown the way to improve their answers to these questions. Some of the questions come from actual examination papers or specimen materials published by Examination Boards. Other questions have been written by Examiners and aim to mirror closely real examination questions set by Examination Boards. The questions meet the requirements of all British Examination Boards.

- There are **sample answers** to some of the questions. They are not perfect answers but they point the way forward for you and perhaps they challenge you to do better. We would suggest that you might consider having a go at some of the tasks before reading the sample answers and then comparing what you have written with the sample answer. Without doubt this will give you food for thought. Remember, though, that there are rarely right or wrong answers in English.

- **Advice from Examiners**. By using the experience of actual Examiners we are able to give advice which can enable the student to see how their answers can be improved and success be ensured.

ASSESSMENT OBJECTIVES IN ENGLISH

Assessment objectives are linked very closely with the **Attainment Targets** of the National Curriculum and it is easiest to look at them in detail by linking them with those Attainment Targets.

Objective 1: Speaking and Listening

- You must be able to demonstrate that you can speak about personal experiences and be able to express your views and feelings.

- You must be able to discuss things in a group and show that you can express your own views and also listen to the views of others.

- You must be able to explain things clearly.

- You must be able to demonstrate that you can work with a group to make a presentation.

- You must be able to show that you understand that how you speak may well change according to your audience and your intentions.

- You must use Standard English, which means grammatically correct English.

- You must demonstrate that you can listen carefully and sympathetically to other speakers.

Objective 2: Reading

- You must be able to demonstrate that you have read a wide range of books with insight and engagement. In your writing you must be able to make appropriate references to the texts and you must be able to sustain interpretations of them.

- You must show that you have read material from the media, newspapers and magazines and also material from non-fiction which might include, for instance, travel books and biographies.

- You must be able to show that you can follow an argument, that you can distinguish between fact and opinion and that you understand why things are written in a particular way.

- You must be able to extract information from different texts and use that information.

- You must be able to judge how writers use language to achieve their effects and you must be able to comment on the language.

Objective 3: Writing

- You must show that you can write in different ways for different purposes and can plan your writing, by writing in paragraphs and using correct punctuation.

- You must be able to show that you can use a range of suitable vocabulary.

- You must show that you know how to revise, edit and improve your writing.

- You must be able to use the grammatical structures of Standard English and a wide vocabulary to express your meanings precisely and clearly.

The *Questions and Answers* series helps you to develop skills and your abilities to meet these assessment objectives by use of questions and by examining possible answers and commenting on them. You might refer to the assessment objectives to help you answer the basic question, "What am I required to do?"

EXAMINATION TECHNIQUE

Success in GCSE examinations comes from proper preparation and a positive attitude to the examination. This book is intended to help you overcome "examination nerves" which often come from a fear of not being properly prepared. Examination technique is extremely important and certainly affects your performance. Remember the basics:

- Read the questions carefully.
- Make sure that you watch the time carefully and complete the paper. It is no good answering one question well if you spend so long doing it that you do not answer another question at all.
- Make sure that you answer the right number of questions. Read the rubric on the front of the examination paper carefully and keep it in mind.
- Examination papers usually tell you how many marks are available for each answer. Take notice of this information as the number of marks gives a guide to the importance of the question and often to the amount which you ought to write.
- Remember to leave time to check through your work carefully.

  Use this book for practice and to gain confidence! Good Luck!

English is not the same as maths and science. It is not as if you can revise all that you have learnt in the hope that the topics will appear in questions on the exam paper.

However, you can so easily throw marks away in English exams by being careless or slovenly. The idea of these revision summaries is to help you eliminate all those silly errors. The aim is to help you to become accurate. Use the summaries to remind you of some of the approaches you need to perform well in written tasks, and of some of the technical points in the composition of writing, but remember that you will only be accurate if you make an effort to get things right in your own work.

SPELLING

You are not allowed to take a dictionary or spell-check into the examinations, but you should use them when you are doing your coursework.

You cannot be expected to spell every word in the English language correctly. However, regular use of a dictionary during your course will help you to master spelling.

Half the battle with accurate spelling is to avoid **careless** errors. To put this point another way, it is important that **you should want to get spellings right!** Be aware of careless errors; check over your work; always be thinking about spellings. At the very least this may help you to cut down the number of errors you make.

There are some very basic spellings which cause confusion. Sometimes they are spellings of words which sound similar but in fact mean something very different. Here are some examples of simple words which are often misspelt:

there, they're, their,

wear, we're, were, where,

no, know, now,

it's, its,

how, who,

whose, who's.

You are going to create a very poor impression if you make these simple errors. Make sure you have learnt the differences. Here are examples to help you learn them:

There are important exams next week. The pupils taking the exams hope **they're** going to pass.

They have been told that they will get **their** results in the Summer.

Cricketers **wear** whites for the match.

The commentator said, "Let's hope **we're** in for a good match!"

Where is the match being played?

Everybody will **know** about the party. There will be **no** food left over.

Now the music can start.

It's nearly time for the holidays.

The school finished **its** term early. (Some hopes!)

How easy is it to play tennis? There are some people **who** will say that it is very easy.

It was difficult to decide **whose** service was better.

I am sure that she is the player **who's** going to win.

Write out one example for each of these simple words, in order to make sure that you can get them right.

To move towards the higher grades in English you need to be able to use an appropriate and extensive vocabulary. You also need to be able to write in the form of Standard English, which will affect your choice of vocabulary. This section is presented as some questions and answers to help you think about vocabulary.

What can I do to develop my vocabulary in a piece of writing?
Always be thinking of alternatives. Never just accept the first word that comes to mind. Never use words sloppily, which do not mean much (e.g. "get" or "nice").

What is meant by "appropriate" vocabulary?
This means choosing the right tone of word. For a report or a formal letter you should not use colloquialisms or slang ("well-good" or "wicked"). Indeed in this kind of writing you should try to be as precise as possible. In a more imaginative piece you might well choose to use colloquialisms or slang, for effect.

What else can I do to achieve an appropriate vocabulary?
Try to vary your use of words, and avoid repetition, especially in the same sentence or paragraph. Remember that by using adjectives (words which describe nouns) and adverbs (words which describe verbs, usually ending in -ly), you can add to the precision of your writing.

How can I extend my vocabulary?
By becoming more interested in the meanings of words, usually through wide reading. In the period approaching your exam, why not read the newspaper for interest? You may have a lot of work to do, but continue reading books, right up to the last minute before your exam. You will continue to take in vocabulary.

Now for a word or two about **clichés**. A cliché is an overworked phrase or word. It is the sort of thing which has been said or written hundreds of times before, and, as a result, when you use it it does not mean anything. Stories sometimes start with: "It was a bright summer day… " Can you see why this is a cliché? Or: "The clouds looked like cotton wool… ".

How can I avoid clichés in my writing?
This will depend on the kind of writing that you are doing. If it is an imaginative piece, try to picture precisely what you are describing. Always try to visualise your events or scenes. If it is an informative piece, try to be clear precisely what you are arguing or stating. On paper, in rough, or in your head, go over the points you are making before you write them down. This should give you a better chance of choosing the most appropriate words.

Should I try to learn new words?
Well, there is no point in forcing out words onto the page if they are just there for effect! That can appear silly. There is a lot to be said for using a thesaurus, however, especially when doing coursework. Above all, a thesaurus can make you enthusiastic for new words.

When you write you need to use paragraphs for TWO main reasons:

❶ your ideas must be organised;

❷ you will make it easier for the reader to follow what you are writing (how important is this in an exam?!)

What is a paragraph?
A paragraph is a section of writing. Writers stop after they have covered a point, or a series of related points, and at a suitable moment, start a new section. When we write in handwriting, which we always do in an exam, we **indent** the start of our new paragraphs. (You will find that this

happens in books although increasingly writers using word processors are not indenting in all documents.) **YOU MUST INDENT!!** However, there is an exception: there is no need to indent the **first paragraph** of a story or essay.

What do we mean by indent? Look at where I positioned the "w" in the first word of this sentence. What do you notice about it? It is slightly moved in from the margin. If you find it difficult to remember to do this, you could also leave a line between one paragraph and the next. You will find helpful examples of the layout of paragraphs in the extracts from the Stimulus material and Exam practice sections of this book. Have a good look at these and make sure you understand how paragraphs are set out.

What do you need to do to make sure that you are using paragraphs?

❶ Use your plan. You do not necessarily need to number each paragraph but it helps if you have been able to **jot down your points in a sequence** which can then form each paragraph. Keep looking back at your plan as this can provide you with a guide for your paragraphs.

❷ As you are writing, think about the **organisation of ideas, events, descriptions, arguments, key points etc.** OK, so it is difficult! A lot of pupils say that they forget to use paragraphs because they are lost in thought. They are too tied up with the ideas in their writing. So try to look up every now and again. **Step back from the page and ask yourself questions about the layout of your work.** I find it helpful to think of it like painting a picture. If your eye is too close to the canvas, you cannot see the whole picture. You need to look at the arrangement of objects in the work, as well as the detail.

How many paragraphs and how often?

There are no easy answers to this question. If you have too many paragraphs and they are then too short, it will suggest that your ideas are too shallow, too simple. On the other hand, overlong paragraphs will make you guilty of inadequate organisation. **You must strike a balance!** One area where you need regular paragraphing is when you are reporting speech in a story. For revision of this see the following revision summary which is on punctuation.

PUNCTUATION

When you write you need to use punctuation for THREE main reasons:

❶ you can show the relationships between one part of a sentence and another;

❷ you can help to stress emphasis or tone in what you are writing;

❸ you will be able to organise your work.

What punctuation do you need to be able to use?

FULL STOPS: to mark the ends of sentences. But do not break down your writing into sentences which are too short! That's too easy!

COMMAS: for a variety of reasons; to mark off one clause from the remainder of the sentence; to establish a pause; to give one word or a few words special emphasis.

CONFUSION BETWEEN FULL STOPS AND COMMAS: sometimes it is easy to confuse the use of commas and full stops. As a general rule any sentence should contain **only one MAIN verb.** If you realise that you are about to start a new "unit of sense", then use a full stop and start a new sentence. Never use a comma loosely when you are really starting a new sentence. However, try to combine or merge sentences to make them more complex – for this you will need the comma regularly.

COLONS AND SEMI-COLONS: Colons (:) are used to introduce lists or to introduce main points of discussion and argument. There are many examples of colons on this page. **Semi-colons** (;) are used to join together two sentences that are very close in their meanings or as a replacement for commas when separating points in a list.

QUESTION MARKS AND EXCLAMATION MARKS: Question marks (?) always end a sentence which asks a question. Note that a question mark contains its own full stop and does not require another one. **Exclamation marks (!)** should be used at the end of a sentence which expresses something very strongly or humorously. But use them sparingly. Too many of them can ruin the effect for the reader.

SPEECH MARKS: also known as **inverted commas** or **quotation marks**, they exist to punctuate **direct** or **reported speech** and also for **titles** and **quotations**. There are some basic guidelines: place the marks at the start and finish of all the speech, including all other marks of punctuation; following the words spoken, when you return to the narrative, continue the sentence – do not use capital letters; if you are reporting the speech of more than one speaker follow the rules of paragraphing, starting each new speaker on a new line and indenting the first words. Remember what was said about paragraphing on pp 5–6.

HYPHENS: for joining words or parts of words; **DASHES:** for separating words or phrases for a particular effect; **BRACKETS:** for marking off phrases or words which are additional to the main sentence (often asides, clarifications, alternatives etc.); **APOSTROPHES:** see the following section.

There are TWO types of apostrophe:

❶ the apostrophe of omission;

❷ the apostrophe of possession.

THE APOSTROPHE OF OMISSION: for use when you are writing a word or combination of words which have been **contracted** and you have left out a letter or more than one letter. This should not be difficult to understand. Simply replace the letter or letters that have been left out with an apostrophe (').

Here are some common contractions in everyday use: it's... he's... we'll... don't... can't.
In each of the above words, which letters have been omitted?
There is another type of omission. This is when you are reporting the way characters speak in a realistic way and you wish to represent accent or dialect.

E.g. 'e's really bin workin' 'ard to pass 'is exams!

THE APOSTROPHE OF POSSESSION (OR POSSESSIVE APOSTROPHE): for use when, in the grammar of your sentence, something belongs to another word, or is literally possessed by another word. This apostrophe is usually called the **apostrophe s**. There are differences between where you place the **apostrophe s** according to whether you have a singular noun "owner" or a plural noun "owner". There is a simple way of remembering the difference. Singular nouns have **'s** and plural nouns have **s'** at the end of the word. Study the difference in the examples below:

For **singular** nouns: The **pupil's** books.
                         The **girl's** pen.

For **plural** nouns: The **athletes'** times. (There is more than one athlete.)
                         The **boys'** games. (There is more than one boy.)

For plural nouns which do not end in "s": The **women's** coats
                                           The **gentlemen's** outfitter.

One word which always causes confusion: its – when you use the word **its** as a possessive pronoun, it does not require a possessive apostrophe. Neither do **his, her, their, our**... so do not be tempted to use one with **its**.

E.g. The dog returns to **its** bone.
     The tree sheds **its** leaves.

See above, in the section on the apostrophe of omission, for the use of the word **it's**.

SPEECH MARKS

1 When the speech comes first:

"There was a huge fire in our road last night," said the worried child.

What to look out for: all the words spoken are contained within the inverted commas; the punctuation (comma) is also contained within the inverted commas; no need for a capital letter after the reported speech – the word "said" simply continues the sentence; the start of the line (paragraph) is indented.

2 When the speech comes second:

The worried child said, "There was a huge fire in our road last night."

What to look out for: again, all the words spoken are contained within the inverted commas; the full stop at the end is contained within the inverted commas; a comma is used to separate the story from the speech (what else could you have used here, instead of a comma?); the start of the line (paragraph) is indented.

3 Mostly speech, a bit of narrative in between:

"There was a huge fire in our road last night," said the worried child, "and there were lots of fire engines!"

4 Other combinations of speech and narrative:

"There was a huge fire in our road last night," said the worried child, "and there were lots of fire engines! You could see the flames right up in the sky." Then she suddenly seemed to remember something important: "but nobody was hurt," she added.

5 When you have more than one speaker:

"There was a huge fire in our road last night," said the worried child, "and there were lots of fire engines!"

"What caused it?" asked his friends.

"I don't know. There are rumours about arson," he replied.

What to look out for: most importantly, notice that each new speaker is given a new line, indented, as each new line is a new paragraph.

Which to use, single (' ') or double (" ") inverted commas?

It is entirely up to you! But remember, whichever you choose, be consistent throughout a piece of work. You cannot vary between single and double – that would be very poor style.

USEFUL TERMS

There are a number of technical terms about language which are helpful in both reading and writing. In responses to reading – comprehensions, appreciations of literature, etc. you may need to use some of the terms, and they may also help you with your own writing. This list includes the basic **parts of speech**.

You will also be aware that you are marked in some sections of your exams for **knowledge about language**. This sometimes involves the use of technical terms to identify and describe features of language. The terms are listed alphabetically here:

Accent: a regional manner of pronunciation.

Acronym: an abbreviation, often instantly recognisable, usually formed from a combination of the first letters of a group of words. Sometimes acronyms are pronounced by their letters (AA, GCSE, RE, The UN, The USA, etc.), sometimes by a word that becomes formed by the first letters of the sequence of words (NATO), and sometimes by a combination of letters (OXFAM).

Adjective: a word used to describe or qualify a noun. Adjectives can express various features, e.g. quality (*big, small, rough, smooth*), quantity (*many, six*), distinguishing features (a *terraced* house, as opposed to a *detached* house).

Adverb: a word used to describe or qualify a verb. Adverbs often end in the letters *ly*. (He ran *quickly*, she walked *briskly*) – but there are many exceptions (He moved *sideways*, she ran *forward*, they were *often* late). Adverbs also serve the purpose of qualifying adjectives (He was *definitely* late, she was *beautifully* tanned),and other adverbs (She ran *extremely* quickly, he walked *very* slowly).

Alliteration: repetition of consonants, commonly used in poetry, to create an effect associated with meaning (*He spoke; the spirits from the sails descend* – "The Rape of the Lock", by Alexander Pope, l.137).

Ambiguity: double meanings – often writers deliberately want to suggest or imply more than one meaning in a phrase or word (*see also* irony).

Analogy: a comparison which does not use imagery – writers often describe a situation or event which is comparable to another one, the effect being that we can then understand the second situation more clearly (e.g. a story about tragic young love might be *analogous* to the story of *Romeo and Juliet*).

Argument essay: writing which presents points of view or opinion, usually backed up by facts and evidence.

Assonance: a combination of vowel sounds, commonly used in poetry, in order to add to the meaning (*The morning-dream that hover'd o'er her head* – "The Rape of the Lock", by Alexander Pope, l. 22).

Attitude: the outlook or point of view held by a writer.

Audience: now a commonly used term to mean "reader" – writers with a clear sense of audience are able to ask the key questions: who am I writing for and for what purpose? – they will then be able to use the most appropriate style, tone or register. The term is particularly useful if you are writing for a clear group of readers, e.g. a story for young children, a set of rules for school, a letter to the newspaper to complain about an issue. But it is not always a useful term – sometimes we just write for ourselves, or for a very general purpose, with no particular audience in mind.

Ballad: a poem that tells a story. Ballads often rhyme, and are frequently associated with traditional stories, sometimes based on legend, often derived from old folk tales with romantic, supernatural or other atmospheric settings.

Blank verse: unrhymed poetry.

Characterisation: how a writer will use language to build up and reveal characters (e.g. through speech, description of appearance, actions, etc.).

Clause: a distinct part of a sentence – as opposed to *phrases*, which are often just a few words. Clauses form units of meaning, like a sentence within a sentence, always with one main verb.

Cliché: a tired, habitually overworked phrase (see p5 for examples).

Colloquialisms: words or phrases which are informal, familiar, part of everyday speech, rather than appropriate in formal styles of writing – try to avoid colloquialisms in more formal writing, but you can use them to good effect, providing they fit the style, in more imaginative pieces.

Conjunction: a joining or linking word in a sentence (*and, or, but, because, if, though*, etc.).

Connotation: a word which carries with it a suggested or implied meaning – names of animals often hold connotations (pig, fish, snake, etc.) – that is, the words have come to hold associations for us other than just as animals.

Derivation: the origins of words.

Description: language used to create a picture of places, people, objects, moods, etc. – some might say that all parts of literature are, by their nature, descriptive, but some passages are brought more vividly to life by a writer's careful use of detail.

Dialect: local variation of standard English.

Dialogue: two or more characters speaking with each other. Note also how important speech is in literature to create characters.

Diction: the choice of words to give a particular slant to meanings – consider, for example, the differences suggested by these words: pupil/student; spectator/fan; storm/tempest.

Direct speech: speech reported in writing (see p8).

Drafting: the process of writing – early stages, through to refining ideas, then final copy, including proof-reading and editing.

Empathy: the ability of a writer to relate to an experience outside their own – to get into somebody else's mind or experiences; this is a skill commonly required in your writing at GCSE – frequently you are asked to take on the role of a particular character.

Evocation (evoke/evocative): the capacity of a writer to bring to life certain memories, feelings, associations – sometimes to call up a certain mood or atmosphere, or a sense of place.

Figurative language: non-literal use of language, often in the form of imagery, but sometimes as figures of speech, e.g. in sayings or proverbs (*a bird in the hand is worth two in the bush ... out of the frying pan, into the fire*).

Formal and **informal registers:** a formal register of language will be marked out by complete sentences, precise vocabulary, complex grammar, and an informal register might use colloquialisms, slang, shortened sentences, in writing which will seem more like conversation.

Genre: a type or collection of writing, e.g. romantic, realistic novel, gothic, fable, ballad, satire – the key thing is that to belong to a genre, a work will contain certain distinguishing features marking it out as a particular type of writing.

Grammar: the construction of language.

Hero: the principal character in a novel or play; usually to be a hero we expect the main character to be a decent sort of character, one who can be admired or held in high esteem.

Hyperbole: exaggeration – to coin a modern phrase, this is when writers "go over the top" with their use of language, suggesting that something is the strongest, the best, the greatest, which of course distorts the truth, (Here is another example from "The Rape of the Lock": *Belinda smiled, and all the world was gay.*).

Idiom: a phrase or expression in current use – often like colloquialisms, these will be familiar, or conversational, or even figurative (*Nice weather for the ducks ... She gave me a piece of her mind*).

Imagery: a non-literal contrast. There are three common types of images used: (examples are again taken from "The Rape of the Lock"):

> **Similes:** *her eyes*
> *like the sun, shine on all alike*
> (a simile makes a comparison by stating that one thing is like another).

Metaphors: in another part of the poem, the writer refers to a pair of scissors:

The little engine on his fingers ends ...

(a metaphor allows the object simply to become what it is being compared with, so in this case the scissors become the little engine, and there is no need for the writer to state that they are like the engine – in this way a metaphor is a more direct comparison).

Personification: this involves turning an object – either inanimate or from nature, into a human or animal form, with human or animal actions and feelings. Pope is here writing about the River Thames:

Thames with pride surveys his rising towers.

It is essential to understand what is meant by *non-literal* language: eyes cannot literally be the sun; a pair of scissors cannot literally be an engine; a river cannot literally survey towers with pride!

Intonation: stress placed on different words, syllables, etc – used to emphasise key points – often termed the "punctuation of speech".

Irony: irony is saying, or writing, one thing, and meaning another; think of it as a form of sarcasm – sometimes people are "put down", for example we might say "well done" to somebody who trips over some steps. Irony in literature is much the same, and is quite often intended to make fun of characters, reveal their weaknesses, or to mock them – so to find ironic language, look for hidden or double meanings.

Jargon: a sort of vocabulary known mostly to particular groups, e.g. of workers – "buzzwords" or an "in-language", maybe used exclusively.

Mockery: speech used ironically, perhaps sarcastically, to create humour.

Monologue: the opposite of dialogue– a character speaking aloud to him or herself.

Mood: often used nowadays to mean tone or atmosphere – you may be asked to describe the mood of some writing: is it sad, tragic, positive, optimistic, romantic, or what? Often you can see how mood has been created by analysing the use of adjectives and adverbs.

Narrator: the teller of a story; we often talk of "**the narrator's voice**" – who is telling the story?; does the teller of the story play a part in it?; is it written in the **first person**, or the **third person**, by the **omniscient narrator**? All of this makes up **narrative technique** – the ways in which a story is written.

Noun: that part of speech which is object (*knife*), thing (*gas*), place (*city*), abstraction (*happiness*), state (*death*), event (*game*), person (*mother*). **Proper nouns** are names or titles (*The Cup Final, John, London*, etc.).

Onomatopoeia: a word used to suggest its meaning by its sound – such as *crash* or *scream*, although clearly, in poetry, the effect will be less obvious, as in this, another example from "The Rape of the Lock": *Now lap-dogs give themselves the rousing shake.* (l.15)

Plot: the plan of events in a story or play – effectively the plot is what happens, as opposed to the subject or themes.

Pronoun: words such as *I, you, he, she, we, they, which, whose* – all words which replace nouns (or more accurately, which replace noun phrases).

Prose: the best way to define prose is to think of it as that writing which is *not* poetry; it is most commonly the writing in stories and novels, and will be characterised by the use of continuous sentences and paragraphs, but it is difficult to give a precise definition.

Pun: a play on words, involving double meanings, sometimes using homophones – words that sound the same, but with different meanings and perhaps different spellings. Shakespeare used a lot of these sorts of puns. *Julius Caesar* begins with a famous one: A citizen of Rome is asked what his job is, and he, a cobbler, jokingly replies that he is a "mender of bad *soles*" – can you see the pun, or double meaning, suggested by the sound of the word?

A lot of modern newspaper headlines are full of puns, often where there is an association of meanings between words: FAMOUS CRICKETER GIVEN BAIL ... POLICEMAN JOINS BEAT GROUP ... VICAR IS PREY OF LOCAL THUGS ... think of your own!

Realism: writing which shows life as it really is – frequently writing which captures a sense of the truth, almost like a photograph or descriptive painting. The effect is often created by mention of down to earth objects, recognisable features, or dialogue which can almost be heard as if spoken aloud.

Register: an increasingly common term, used to mean the type of language being used in any particular situation; perhaps the best way to define register is by the word *variety* – possible different registers are: literary, poetic, formal, informal, presentational, gossip, argumentative, lecture, discursive, informative, persuasive ... but really the list is endless.

Rhetoric: nowadays we tend to use this term to mean persuasive, frequently elegant language, used in speeches and argument. Sometimes it is used as a way of criticising a speaker by implying that he has used words powerfully and convincingly, but without much substance in the argument. In the past, rhetoric more accurately meant "the art of speech-making".

Rhyme: words placed in a relationship in poetry, frequently at the ends of lines, due to their sounding the same, e.g.

> Behold, four kings in majesty *revered*,
> With hoary whiskers and a forky *beard*.   "The Rape of the Lock", l. 37-8.

Rhythm: the metre, or the beat of lines in poetry.

Satire: mockery in literature, intended to poke fun at characters, in order to expose their weaknesses, their foolishness, or their immorality; the best way to think of satire is to think of the popular television programme, *Spitting Image*.

Slang: alternative words used by groups of people, often all from the same area

Standard English: the form of written and spoken English generally agreed as most appropriate for use in public contexts, e.g.work, formal communications, business, education, journalism, etc.

Soliloquy: a speech in a play spoken by one character to the audience only – really a character thinking aloud; a technique used a great deal by Shakespeare.

Style: that part of literature which is to do with the expression, as opposed to the content, ideas, themes or subject matter – style is always associated with *how* literature is written rather than *what* it is about.

Symbol: the use of one thing to represent or suggest something else, in literature. We talk about objects or events being symbolic of a mood, feeling or idea, even if, at first glance they do not appear related.

Syntax: the way that sentences are constructed.

Themes: connected ideas which arise in literature, often revealed through the actions of more than one character, a number of events, or with features of the language which are expressed more than once – we might discover themes of love, fate, power, despair, innocence, evil, all to be interpreted from different parts of a work of literature. Some of the main themes in Shakespeare's plays would be: "Romeo and Juliet": *impatience*; "A Midsummer Night's Dream": *mischief*; "Julius Caesar": *honour*.

Tone: the overall mood or feeling of language, for example the tone could be humorous, tragic, persuasive, sympathetic, mocking, serious, etc.

Verb: many young children are taught that verbs are "doing words", but this definition is now rejected as inadequate; more strictly, a verb is a "happening" or "occurring" word – the word(s) needed for something to take place in a sentence. Sentences cannot be formed without verbs, they would end up making no sense, as would be the case in the following example:

> The athlete *won* the race.
>
> Remove the verb, and see what you are left with:
>
> The athlete the race.

Vocabulary: the variety and selection of words; it is an important skill to extend your vocabulary, and the best way to do this is by using a thesaurus.

Voice: now a common term used to mean "the writer's sense of presence in a piece of writing" – you have probably been told by your teachers to "put something of yourself into your writing". This is achieved by being interested in what you have to say, so that there is evidence that you as a writer are genuinely expressing yourself.

This section aims to remind you of the range of **types of writing** that you need to be able to do in English exams. Writing is a very varied sort of activity. You need to be able to distinguish between the different demands of writing imaginatively, writing formally, writing to inform or to describe, writing personally, and writing for a particular audience.

There is also reference to **reading** and **understanding** skills in this section. It is, after all, very rare that we write without involving ourselves in reading, and responding to what we read. Try not to separate reading and writing in your mind. Think of one as dependent on the other.

WRITING TO INFORM, EXPLAIN AND DESCRIBE

One type of writing which you are required to do, no matter which syllabus you are studying, is writing to inform, explain or describe.

Here are two poems by Seamus Heaney. In both cases the poems talk about the poet's father and their relationship. You will be asked to write informatively and descriptively.

STIMULUS MATERIAL

Follower

My father worked with a horse-plough,
His shoulders globed like a full sail strung
Between the shafts and the furrow.
The horses strained at his clicking tongue.

5 An expert. He would set the wing
And fit the bright steel-pointed sock.
The sod rolled over without breaking.
At the headrig, with a single pluck

Of reins, the sweating team turned round
10 And back into the land. His eye
Narrowed and angled at the ground,
Mapping the furrow exactly.

I stumbled in his hob-nailed wake,
Fell sometimes on the polished sod;
15 Sometimes he rode me on his back
Dipping and rising to his plod.

I wanted to grow up and plough,
To close one eye, stiffen my arm.
All I ever did was follow
20 In his broad shadow around the farm.

I was a nuisance, tripping, falling,
Yapping always. But today
It is my father who keeps stumbling
Behind me, and will not go away.

Digging

Between my finger and my thumb
The squat pen rests; snug as a gun.

Under my window, a clean rasping sound
When the spade sinks into gravelly ground:
5 My father, digging. I look down

Till his straining rump among the flowerbeds
Bends low, comes up twenty years away
Stooping in rhythmn through potato drills
Where he was digging.

10 The coarse boot nestled on the lug, the shaft
Against the inside knee was levered firmly.
He rooted out tall tops, buried the bright edge deep
To scatter new potatoes that we picked
Loving their cool hardness in our hands.

15 By God, the old man could handle a spade.
Just like his old man.

My grandfather cut more turf in a day
Than any other man on Toner's bog.
Once I carried him milk in a bottle
20 Corked sloppily with paper. He straightened up
To drink it, then fell to right away

Nicking and slicing neatly, heaving sods
Over his shoulder, going down and down
For the good turf. Digging.

25 The cold smell of potato mould, the squelch and slap
Of soggy peat, the curt cuts of an edge
Through living roots awaken in my head.
But I've no spade to follow men like them.

Between my finger and my thumb
30 The squat pen rests.
I'll dig with it.

Write a short piece, no more than one side in length, of a biography of either your father or an adult who you know well, You may use some of the ideas and approaches from the poems to help you.

TASK

Examiner's tip This is a fairly open task and could really be treated in a number of ways. An examiner would be interested to see how well you manage to develop ideas and attitudes in a piece of biographical writing, rather than just providing a catalogue of facts or events in someone's life.

The writing should involve a strong personal commitment and engagement, and the best pieces might use a range of techniques, including some description of appearance as well as action, and perhaps some comment. A sense of audience is important – remember that you are using explanation and description to bring the character to life for a reader who will not know who you are writing about.

Although the question does not require you to use the ideas and approaches in Seamus Heaney's two poems, it would be advisable to do so. In the answer published below, this candidate has successfully brought out her feelings about her father and thought about their relationship, through a description of him at work, using similar ideas to those in the poems.

ANSWER

BIOGRAPHY OF MY FATHER

He has always had green wellingtons, my father. He did not always wear them – I remember the father of my youth as a giant, a bad-tempered one, who only came home as the skies darkened and the diamond-dust lit up to wink its warning above our heads – but they were always there, his boots, to trip our small feet as we squeezed past them out of the back door. His home-coming used to tear me away from the neon appeal of the television and send me cowering up here, to my room, while he told my mother what was wrong today. But circumstances change, and time has mellowed him, so I now like to come up here and watch as he turns over turf to be ready for next spring's planting. On a Sunday the disregarded radio plays, someone's hard-written script burbling unnoticed behind him. I think he leaves it there for company: the contented spewing of formless words helps him beat the land into the shape of his flowered fancies.

I cannot share his hobby: the back-breakin monotony of the wounding spade bores me, and I could not be contented with it. But, as I see him alone down there, I think I envy nature's possession of him and his green wellington boots.

15

You are sometimes asked to write imaginatively, possibly a story. You might just be given a title which you are free to interpret in any way you like. You might be given an extract of narrative writing to give you ideas for your own writing.

In this case, before getting down to your writing, you should think of what you have discovered about the two characters, what might happen which is consistent with what you have learnt about the characters, and what you should do to copy Ewan Clarkson's style of writing.

What you are going to read now is an extract from a novel. The task which follows asks you to write in an imaginative and entertaining way.

ICE TREK by EWAN CLARKSON
(Two very different men are stranded together after a plane crash.)

Suddenly Larsen remembered his knife. It was the sort of penknife beloved of small boys, no more than a toy, an intricate maze of folding blades and gadgets, all wholly impractical but delightfully ingenious. He produced it for Umiak's inspection.

He had expected ridicule. Instead Umiak stared at it intently, and then began a prolonged and meticulous examination, testing every blade and gadget, opening and closing each one several times.

They found a use for it straight away, converting the gallon can into a petrol stove, using dry sand from beside the stream. Together they designed it, cutting a flap of metal from one side of the can, but leaving it hinged to act as a windshield or perhaps, they hoped, a hot-plate. They had trouble draining petrol from the fuel tank of the plane but at last they had about half a gallon in a plastic bag. The fire burned well but, to Larsen's chagrin, with a sooty black flame which Umiak explained was caused by seal oil from the can. Umiak suggested a drink of hot water but Larsen remained frustrated as there appeared to be nothing to boil it in.

Umiak sat silent for a while. Then he got up and began pottering among the stones. Larsen sat on alone, hunched over the flames of the stove, straining his ears in the hope of hearing a plane. There was nothing, no sound save that of Umiak clattering among the rocks. The valley was devoid of life, and not even a raven showed in the sky above the crags.

His reverie was interrupted by Umiak, who appeared at his side with a handful of round flat pebbles, which he proceeded to pile on the stove. Then he squatted back on his heels, watching the flames play over the stones. Nearby he had built a nest of rocks and moss, lining it with a plastic bag which he had half filled with water. When he judged the pebbles hot enough he deftly shovelled them out of the flames, using two flat slates he had chosen for the purpose. Swiftly he transferred them to the water, which hissed and bubbled as the stones sank. In a few moments the water was too hot to touch.

Umiak dipped the cup in the water and offered it to Larsen. The brew did not look inviting. The stones had blackened with carbon from the residue of the seal oil, and bits of it had floated on the surface. Despite Umiak's insistence Larsen was not tempted. He was tired of lessons in survival and Umiak, sensing this, drained the cup and then sat silent. The white man depressed him. Umiak wandered down the valley. Alone he knew he could survive, and this knowledge, blended with an instinctive love of the land of which he felt so much a part, left no room in his mind for fear or concern.

The presence of the white man did though. There was a fundamental difference between the two races, in their attitude to the world around them. For ten thousand years his people had learned to live with the land, and to make the best use of all it had to offer. At some point during that time the white men, the strangers, had chosen not to adapt their ways to natural cycles, and instead had learned to domesticate stock and to cultivate crops. From that point on they had been compelled more and more to fight against the forces of the wild.

In the days to come Larsen would grow to need him. The man was not yet prepared to accept this, and Umiak was not sure how to convince him without antagonising him. On the other hand he did not need Larsen.

TASK

"In the days to come Larsen would grow to need him." Write a continuation which shows what you think did happen.

UCLES 1993

Examiner's tip

One thing which is essential here is that you really get into the extract and understand the characters. Larsen and Umiak are very different having been raised in different cultures and Umiak clearly stands a far better chance of coping than Larsen.

Their relationship could clearly develop at one of two extremes, complete antagonism or mutual trust; or the development could be somewhere in between. You must decide what is most likely.

Do not forget to use the passage. In considering what is likely to happen you must consider what has already happened as your writing must be a logical progression.

You must also consider the style in which the extract is written. You have been asked to write a continuation and you should therefore be making an attempt to write in the same style. You should, for instance, look at the type of vocabulary which has been used. You might also look at the sentence structure; for instance many of the sentences in the extract are quite short and succinct and there are few long complex sentences.

ANSWER

Shahzad Hussain.

ICE TREK

– CONTINUATION

In the days to come Larsen would grow to need him. Umiak knew that he himself could survive until help arrived but Larsen on his own had no chance of survival.

Later on Umiak decided to put a proposal to Larsen saying that Larsen would cooperate with Umiak or they would go their own separate ways. Larsen somewhat surprised at Umiaks proposal, hastily agreed to cooperate.

Just by the sound of his voice Umiak knew that Larsen was not prepared to do anything. Larsen just sitting there fiddling with his penknife depressed Umiak. Umiak snatched the knife out of his hands and took it inside the wreckage. Larsen intrigued by this immediately got up and followed Umiak inside the remains of the plane. There he saw Umiak with his knife cutting off the foam and sponge of the chair. Larsen seeing this stopped and realised what a fool he had been degrading Umiak and thinking of him as the lower human being. He was a sea of knowledge, boiling water with rocks and a plastic bag, his knowledge was vital for survival. One way or another he would have to cooperate.

Then after his long thoughts, Larsen immediately proceeded towards Umiak and seeing Umiak feeling tired and weary took the knife from his hands and started collecting the foam and sponge. Umiak observing this felt a great sense of relief and a smile appeared across his face.

After a little while, Umiak and Larsen taking turns to collect the sponge, had a great big heap of sponge. They together went round the wreckage seeing the best place for shelter. It seemed as though their differences had all of a sudden had been resolved.

Umiak started to bring the sponge to the appointed place and spreading evenly the sponge among the ground. A good friendship was about to start. Well written with a nice tone – well done (A)

NEW CHAPTER.

WRITING TO ANALYSE, REVIEW AND COMMENT

The third type of writing which is referred to in the GCSE syllabus is to analyse, review and comment. Here you are asked to produce such a piece of writing.

Printed below is a piece of writing from the June 1995 edition of the Reader's Digest which talks about an aspect of smoking. It is a fact that smoking is again on the increase among young people.

STIMULUS MATERIAL

How cigarettes cloud your brain

by Lowell Ponte

Let's say you're a smoker, lighting up your first cigarette of the day. Within moments you start to feel the mind-altering changes smoking brings.

Almost everyone, including those who do it, acknowledges the long-term health risks of smoking, especially lung cancer and coronary heart disease. But most smokers perceive the immediate effect of smoking as positive: a stimulant that makes them feel more alert, clear headed and able to focus on work.

But does smoking really have these effects? No: the smoker's perception is mostly an illusion. Take a close look at what smoke does to the brain.

Within ten seconds of your first inhalation, nicotine, a potent alkaloid, passes into your bloodstream, crosses the barrier that protects the brain from most impurities, and begins to act on brain cells. Nicotine molecules fit like keys into the "nicotinic" receptors on the surface of the brain's receptors on the surface of the brain's neurons.

In fact, nicotine fits the same "keyholes" as one of the brain's most important neurotransmitters (signal chemicals), acetylcholine. By mimicking acetylcholine, the 1.5 milligrammes of nicotine obtained from smoking your first cigarette elicit the body's excitation chemicals, including adrenalin (epinephrine) and noradrenalin (norepinephrine). This gives you a rush of stimulation and increases the flow of blood in your brain.

If an electronencephalograph were wired to your head, your EEG would almost immediately record a change in brainwave patterns. Your brain's output of alpha waves electrical impulses associated with alert relaxation – dips at first but is restored by the time you finish your first cigarette. The sleep-related delta waves and theta waves – involved in emotions, creative imagery and deep thought – grow weaker. But your brain's electrical output surges in beta waves, typically seen during intense concentration and mental agitation.

TEN puffs have flowed through your lungs, and that first cigarette has burned to ash. You feel energised and clear-headed. Are you more sharply focused now than,

say, a non-smoking colleague? You may think so, but your improved state of mind is partly due to the fact that you've just ended a period of nicotine deprivation. And you're about to enter another.

Within 30 minutes, the nicotine you've ingested is sharply reduced, and you feel your energy begin to slip away. You light a second cigarette. Again you feel an adrenalin surge, but now the experience is subtly different.

Nicotine triggers a cascade of biochemical changes in the brain. A stress-regulating substance called cortisol is released, along with beta-endorphin, the brain's opiate-like pain reliever. With this second cigarette you begin to feel one of the paradoxes of smoking – that at one dose it can stimulate, at another soothe. You feel muscles throughout your body start to relax, and your pain threshold rises.

THIRTY more minutes pass, and your attention increasingly drifts away from your work and towards that nearby packet of cigarettes. The craving smokers feel for nicotine is more than psychological, more than a habit or a desire of the kind people feel for chocolate. Nicotine prompts brain cells to grow many more nicotinic receptors than they would otherwise. This allows the brain to function normally despite an unnatural amount of acetylcholine-like chemical acting on it. Nicotine thus reshapes the brain so that a smoker feels normal when nicotine floods his or her neurons and abnormal when it doesn't.

Most smokers are engaged in a daily struggle, says Jonathan Foulds, specialist in Tobacco Addiction at St George's Hospital Medical School in London. "They need a constant supply of Nicotine to avoid the poor concentration of withdrawal and in many offices, restaurants, trains and so on, this is unacceptable and must be done covertly. The smokers can't relax."

The American Psychiatric Association classifies smoking withdrawal as a "nicotine-induced organic mental disorder" whose symptoms include anxiety, irritability, anger, restlessness, frustration, insomnia, decreased heart rate and increased appetite.

Several studies have compared active smokers with "deprived" smokers – those suffering nicotine withdrawal – on their ability to perform simple skill tests. These are often cited (and many were funded)

by the tobacco industry as evidence that smoking enhances alertness and performance. "What they really show," says Jack Henningfield of the US National Institute on Drug Abuse, "is that nicotine withdrawal causes dramatic mental dysfunction".

IT'S no later than mid-morning when you light your third cigarette. Compared with the first, it tastes flat. If you're like most of the 12.5 million adult Britons who still smoke, you will soon be lighting the next and the next almost by reflex. Smokers average 15 cigarettes a day, meaning nearly 55,000 inhalations a year.

Besides the nicotine, those puffs obtain carbon monoxide. This gas robs the smoker of oxygen by bonding – at least 200 times more tightly than oxygen does – to the haemoglobin that ordinarily delivers oxygen to cells throughout the body. Because of the carbon monoxide, cells cannot prise oxygen atoms loose. If a significant percentage of your haemoglobin were thus made useless by carbon monoxide, you would almost certainly die.

Each cigarette pumps ten to 20 milligrammes of carbon monoxide into your lungs. People typically lose three to nine per cent of their oxygen carrying capacity while smoking. During periods of intense smoking, this loss can reach more than ten per cent, which may slow reaction time and reduce mental awareness.

PSYCHOLOGIST George Spilich and colleagues at Washington College in Maryland decided to find out whether, as many smokers say, smoking helps them to "think and concentrate". Spilich put young non-smokers, active smokers and smokers deprived of cigarettes through a series of tests.

In the first, each subject sat before a computer screen and pressed the space-bar as soon as he or she recognised a target letter among an array of 96. In this simple test, smokers, deprived smokers and non-smokers performed equally well.

The next test was more complex, requiring all to scan sequences of 20 identical letters and respond the instant one of the letters transformed into a different one. Non-smokers were fastest, but under the stimulation of nicotine, active smokers were faster than

deprived smokers.

The complexity of the test increased. A third test required people to remember a sequence of letters or numbers and respond when that sequence appeared amid flashed groupings on the screen. In this test of short-term memory, non smokers made the fewest errors, but deprived smokers committed fewer errors than active smokers.

The fourth experiment required people to read a passage, then answer questions about it. Non-smokers remembered 19 per cent more of the most important information than active smokers, and deprived smokers bettered their counterparts who had smoked cigarette just before testing. Active smokers not only tended to have poorer memories but also had trouble differentiating important information from trivial details.

From his final experiment, Spilich got subjects to perform in a computer-generated driving simulator, much like a quick-paced video game. Participants had to operate a steering-wheel, gear lever and accelerator pedal, and cope with unexpected challenges such as twisting roads, the sudden appearance of cars and oil-slicks. By the end of the test, deprived smokers were involved in roughly 67 per cent more rear-end collisions than nonsmokers. Smokers who had just had a cigarette did even worse. They were involved in significantly more simulated accidents and three and a half times more rear-end collisions than were non-smokers.

"As our test became more complex," sums up Spilich, "the non-smokers outperformed the smokers by wider and wider margins."

On the basis of this research, Spilich speculates, "a smoker might perform adequately at many jobs – until they got complicated. He could drive a car satisfactorily so long as everything remained routine, but if a tyre blew out at high speed he might not handle the emergency as well as a non-smoker. A smoking airline pilot could fly adequately if no problems arose, but if something went wrong, smoking might impair his mental capacity. If lack of sleep were also a problem, smoking could leave such a pilot relatively impaired - with dangerous consequences."

Consider that the next time you light up the day's first cigarette – and drive your car to work.

Use the information from the article and your own views in writing your own article arguing either for or against smoking.

Examiner's tip It is important to understand the writing skills required here. It's worth just thinking about what they mean. *Review* means making an overall judgement about a topic: in this case, one that you are asked to read about first. It is quite a demanding skill as you are being asked to hold in your mind a number of key ideas all at once. *Analysis* is the skill of examining an issue, of unravelling and interpreting the main points. Then you need to be able to *comment* appropriately on your ideas and findings. This involves making well informed judgements, taking account of the readers so that they can follow your views.

Examiners will want to see evidence of clear planning and organisation, with logical and structured points leading the reader through the main parts of the argument. The writing will need to be relatively formal, with clear progression from one paragraph to another. There will need to be an informed response to the Reader's Digest article and use of mature and relevant ideas from the candidate's own experience of smoking as an issue in society.

Smoking.

Many people when introduced to a cigarette are attracted to it's effects. How can this not be? A greater percentage of people today are aware of it's dangers and still persevere. People are no longer guinea pigs and the effects and dangers of smoking are no longer unforseen. Many, after enjoying this stimulus, have been suffering from it's consequences for years. Smoking is responsible for many deaths, disabilities and illnesses such as Chronic Bronchitis, Emphysema, Cardiovascular disease and lung Cancer.

The smoker is playing Russian Roulette with their life. Cigarette smoke consists of more than 4,700 compounds, 43 of which are Carcinogens, such as tar. Nicotine a poisonous alkaloid is considered the addicting agent that makes quitting so difficult. 50 mg of an alkaloid on an adults tongue is fatal.

Yet smoking is an escape, Sweet nicotine burning through your veins, muscles relaxing. A smoker can sit back and become more sociable. Because at first your in control; the cigarette is just a friend invited into your bloodstream. Alkaloid; a guest in your brain. Yet after time you are slowly seduced as the craving for Nicotine increases. This is how Nicotine works; slowly and slyly it invades your head. Nicotine molecules in deceiving your brain fit perfectly into nicotinic receptor. At first there's a headrush as the increase in adrenalin pumps your blood faster around your body, then there's the feeling of alertness and refreshment. As your body overcomes the nicotine this enjoys energy slips away and your fingers fidget for just one more drag. You can't concentrate or be content until Nicotine is pumping around your blood stream.

Your brain has been manipulated. Alkaloid, unknown to the smoker, has altered your brain by increasing the number of Nicotinic receptors. The smoker only feels normal and in control when Nicotine is in their blood.

Nicotine infests your head, it has control it's no longer a guest. Your brain is now it's habitat. You crave it's effects. Sparking up a cigarette becomes as natural as breathing and depriving the brain of this can cause an altered personality; anxiety, irritability, anger, restlessness, frustration, insomnia and a decreased heart rate can take effect. A smoker has a 'Nicotine-induced organic mental disorder'.

An alkaloid can not only enter the body by inhaling but it can be absorbed into the blood stream via your skin. 40,000 non-smokers die every year in America alone through passive smoking. A lack of respect for yourself can prove fatal to others.

WRITING INFORMATIVELY – A REPORT

Quite often you are given some information and then asked to write a report.

One of the most important things to do before starting to write your report is to ask yourself some questions. What am I writing this report for? Who am I writing this report for? Do I need to use all the information I have been given? Should I add ideas of my own?

What you are now going to read is some information. The task which follows is asking you to write a report.

STIMULUS MATERIAL

DISASTER

Some years ago a dreadful fire occurred at a London Underground station. It was the worst fire in the history of the London Underground. At 7.46p.m. on Wednesday November 18, 1987, a huge ball of flame shot from an escalator shaft across the booking hall at King's Cross Station. Thirty-one people died from the smoke and fire; six more were appallingly injured.

Piecing together the details, an official investigator's notebook contained the following:

FACT   escalators were made of wood/had been in service since 1939;

19.15   inspector in relevant area noticed no problem;

19.17   one man, peering through the gaps between escalator treads saw "a ball of sparks" moving with the escalator/he told the clerk/clerk reported it by telephone;

19.28   passenger pushed the emergency stop button at the top of the escalator/railman saw flames and put tape across the escalator to prevent passengers using it;

19.32   policeman made an alarm call over his radio;

19.36   flames and smoke had spread right across escalator/passengers took no notice – even stepping across the tape/police passed on alarm to fire service;

FACT   only one policeman on duty at ground level;

FACT   for a time trains continued to stop and discharge passengers;

FACT   no officials of the underground railway were on hand to advise;

FACT   passengers found one of the exit gates locked;

19.40   police officers at the foot of the escalators decided to ask for an instruction to be given to prevent trains stopping at the station;

19.42   first fire engines arrive at the station;

19.45   police started directing passengers up unaffected escalators;

19.46   explosion;

NOTE cause of fire was probably a lighted match dropped onto accumulated dirt and grease under the escalator.

TASK

Using the details noted above, imagine you are the official investigator and write a report to the managing director of London Underground. You want to inform him of the facts but you may also wish to make some comments and recommendations.

ANSWER

To the Managing Director London Underground Railway
Report on the fire at King's Cross Station – Wednesday November 18 1987

This report is focused on what I believe was the worst fire in the history of the London Underground. The result of the fire was that thirty one people died from the smoke and fire; six more were appallingly injured and thousands of pounds of damage was done.

The fire took place on the escalator shaft at King's Cross Station, where a fireball shot across the booking hall where many civilians were waiting for a train and collecting their tickets. The escalators were made of wood and had been in service since 1939, so were quite old. The wood caught a light very quickly and flames spread at quite a fast rate – should there have been an updated escalator system? The "ball of sparks" that appeared in the escalator was reported straight away by the clerk by telephone. It was efficiently done. At 19.28, a passenger then pushed the emergency stop button at the top of the escalator – railman saw the flames on escalator and for safety reasons put tape across the escalator.

Precautions were taken by the policemen but flames and smoke had spread right across escalator by 19.36. A lack of authority was shown by policemen and railstaff, as commuters stepped over safety tape. Fire service were called by the police at 19.36 to deal with fire.

Only one policeman had been on duty at ground level when the fire began. I believe that this is not enough to cope with an emergency. The trains were not stopped from stopping at the station immediately after the fire broke out, but continued to stop & discharge people – this was wrong as it endangered the passengers and crowded the area, making it increasingly hard to deal with the emergency services. There were also no officials of the underground railway on hand to advise people, so a lack of knowledge of the situation in hand was present.

The probable cause of the explosion, was a lighted match. I believe that a ban on smoking is also necessary.

N Ashton

WRITING TO PERSUADE – A LETTER

Essentially there are two types of letter which you might be asked to write in an examination. The first is a formal letter and the second a personal letter.

There are differences in the style and layout but in these days of word processing, desk-top publishing and generally improving technology, it is no longer possible to say that there is one right way to lay out a letter and that other ways are wrong.

What we can say is that if you are writing a formal letter it should be headed with your address and the name and address of the person who is to receive the letter. It should be dated and the recipient should be addressed either by name or by a title, "Sir" or "Madam". If you use a name then end the letter "Yours sincerely"; if you use a title then end the letter "Yours faithfully". A most important thing is that your letter looks neat and professional.

If you are writing a personal letter you should put your own address and the date but there is no need to put the recipient's name and address. You may choose to end the letter with "Yours sincerely" but you may also choose to end it more informally.

Below is some information about cigarettes and passive smoking which is taken from a book called *The Environment and Health*. The task, a letter-writing task, follows.

STIMULUS MATERIAL

Cigarettes and passive smoking

Nearly everyone now accepts that cigarette smoking greatly increases the risk of bronchitis, lung cancer or heart disease. But around a third of the adult population continues to smoke, and many young people take up the habit.

Unfortunately, cigarette smoking does not only affect the smoker; it damages the environment and the health of other people too. Just being in a smoky room is the equivalent of smoking one cigarette for every 20 actually being smoked.

The risk seems to be greatest for the families of smokers, and young people are more likely to suffer lung problems if their parents smoke. It is known that the non-smoking wives of male smokers are about a third more likely to develop lung cancer than the non-smoking wives of non-smokers. The smoke drifting from another person's cigarette contains a much worse mixture of damaging chemicals than the smoke the smoker inhales – five times as much carbon monoxide, which can be harmful to the heart and circulation, and about fifty times as much of the cancer-causing chemicals.

There is now no doubt that exposure to other people's cigarette smoke is damaging to health. Lung cancer is more common than usual in non-smokers who work in smoky environments. Children whose parents smoke are more likely to suffer from coughs and respiratory diseases.

Many smokers are not aware of the irritation their habit can cause to non-smokers. Children often grow up in a smoky environment, which can damage their lungs from an early age.

Respiratory illness 5–9 years

Persistent cough 8–19 years

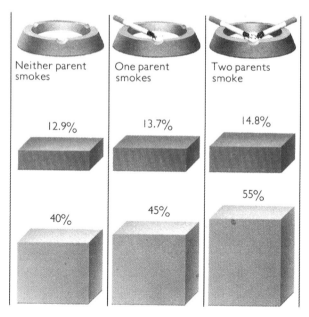

Neither parent smokes — 12.9% — 40%

One parent smokes — 13.7% — 45%

Two parents smoke — 14.8% — 55%

TASK

You have a friend who smokes and you are anxious that they should give up because you believe they are damaging their health. Write a persuasive letter to your friend in which you try to convince her/him that not smoking is better. Use information from the stimulus material to help you form your argument.

Examiner's tip As is so often the case there is a key word here in the task which you must recognise. The word is "persuasive". This should set the tone for the answer. You might start and end the letter in a friendly, informal manner, but the key purpose is to offer clear advice. You are writing with a serious purpose in mind and that purpose is to persuade your friend to give up smoking.

Make sure then that you get the tone right; friendly but sincere and genuine in your concern.

Use points from the information given but add points of your own. (It might be a help if you are able to think of a real friend when you are working out what to say and what the reaction is likely to be when the letter is received.)

ANSWER

> 69. Broome Manor Lane
> Swindon
> Wilts.
> SN3 1NB.
> 31st. July, 1994.
>
> Dear Nicky,
>
> How's it going? Hope you are well — considering the amount you smoke each day! No, I'm not going to lecture, but I am concerned about your smoking habit, especially when you look at the statistics. I just don't understand why you do it when you see your mum with her bronchitis, from smoking for however many years. And you may not be lucky enough to get just bronchitis, you could get lung cancer, or some kind of heart disease. Is that really worth it just to look cool in front of the older guys? And have you ever thought about what you are doing to me. I have to sit there breathing in your smoke for hours on end, I'm just glad I'm not married to you! The other day I found out that the smoke I accidently inhale from your cigarettes contains far more damaging chemicals than the smoke that is going inside of you. So if I end up with cancer then I'll know who to blame.
>
> But, I can't force you to stop, just think about smoking in other peoples company, especially children. You don't want the increase in children having lung cancer on your conscience now do you?
>
> Anyway, lecture over, take care and write back soon.
>
> love
> Becky

23

Responding to different kinds of stimulus material

This section is all about "responding to stimuli" – or, put more simply, doing the tasks set. It is introduced by a basic comprehension test and then different types of stimuli are used, including literary, media and non-fiction. You will find detailed examination tasks (or questions) with some examples of responses (or answers) written by real pupils.

If you really want a challenge, why not have a go at the tasks yourself before you look at the responses of the pupils?

At the end of the section see if you have been able to identify the main principles involved in responding to English exam questions. In English you are never marked for getting answers right or wrong. Using and understanding English – your own language – can never be as simple as that. So try to use this section to grasp what sorts of things you will be marked for.

COMPREHENSION

Comprehension is a general word which means "understanding". In exams you are asked to read passages, and to show that you understand them you are then asked a series of questions about the meanings and language.

It is important that you understand some of the skills involved in answering comprehension questions; what is most important is that you learn how to interpret the types of questions that you are asked.

First, let's look at a comprehension passage and the answers that have been written by one pupil. Read the following passage carefully and then answer the questions that follow. You should try to answer all the questions and, as far as possible, to answer in your own words.

The writer, a travel writer, Michael Palin, is recounting a journey from the North to South Poles. Near the start of his journey, he and his group of travellers are on Day 6, and have reached Kap Wik which is still in the far north. The passage describes his reception at the home of Harald Solheim, who lives near the Arctic Circle.

STIMULUS MATERIAL

DAY 6 KAP WIK TO LONGYEARBYEN

It's 2.45 in the morning when we arrive at Harald Solheim's hut. A tall wooden frame hung with seal carcasses stands on a slight rise, more prominent than the cabin itself, which is set lower down, out of the wind. The first surprise is Harald himself. Instead of some grizzly bearded old-timer, a tall, pale, studious figure comes out to welcome us. He does have a beard, but attached as it is to long, aquiline features the effect is more rabbi than trapper. The second surprise is how benignly and agreeably he copes with the appearance of ten tired and hungry travellers in the middle of the night. First we fill up his miniscule hallway with our boots and bags, then we burst his sitting-room to the seams, whilst he heats up some stew on a wood-burning stove. His wood supply, neatly stacked in a workshop, is driftwood, probably from the Russian coast. His electricity supply is wind-generated.

He fetches out a leg of smoked reindeer which is quite delicious and over this and a mixture of stew, smoked salmon, Aquavit (the local spirit) and Glenmorangie whisky we thaw out and swap stories. Harald offers advice, comment and information, liberally laced with dry humour. It's like some wonderfully chaotic tutorial.

Around about 4.30 a.m. some of us start looking a little anxiously for the dormitory. Harald explains the arrangements. In a next-door room he has four bunk-beds and floor space for two. There is more space on the floor of his workshop. Everyone else will have to sleep in the sitting-room with him. There is one sit-down loo, but as this is a bag that has to be emptied men are requested to use the Great Outdoors whenever possible, but to refrain from peeing on the side

of the house from which he draws his water supply. For cleaning teeth and washing he recommends the snow.

When I wake, it's half-past eleven. The sitting-room resembles some Viking Valhalla with recumbent Norwegians scattered about and Harald sprawled on the sofa like a warrior slain in battle. Then the telephone rings. Last night my tired brain was so busy romanticizing Harald's existence that I hadn't noticed the phone, or the remote control for the matt-black hi-fi, or the visitor's book, or the collection of Rachmaninov piano concertos on CD, signed 'To Harald from Vladimir Askenazy'. Is it all a dream? Have we been hi-jacked in the night to some apartment in Oslo? I stumble outside clutching my toothbrush and there is the reassuring reality of empty mountains and frozen seas stretching as far as the eye can see.

I scrub snow all over my face and neck. A refreshing shock which dispels any lurking hangover. When I get back indoors Harald is off the phone and preparing coffee. This autumn, he tells me, he will be celebrating 15 years at Kap Wik. He has family in Norway, but they don't visit much. His closest neighbours are the Russians at the mining town of Pyramiden, 18 miles away. He reads a lot, 'Almost everything except religious literature' and hunts seal, reindeer, Arctic fox (a pelt will fetch around £80) and snowgeese, ' "Goose Kap Wik" was served to the King and Queen of Norway,' he informs me, with quiet satisfaction.

'So it's a busy life in the middle of nowhere?'

Harald shrugs. 'Some years I don't see a living soul from autumn to July.'

I ask him if he has ever felt the need for companionship. A woman around the house perhaps.

'It's… er…,' he smiles at his sudden inarticulacy… 'it's not easy to explain in Norwegian… but any woman mad enough to come here…'

He never finishes the sentence. The sound of a distant helicopter brings him to his feet.

'It's my mail', he explains, almost apologetically, as a Sea King helicopter clatters into sight across the fiord.

After a late lunch and more stories our caravan is repacked and relaunched. Harald, smiling, waves us away. I don't really understand why a man of such curiosity, fluency and culture should want to chase animals around Spitsbergen, but I feel he rather enjoys being an enigma, and though he is no hermit he is one of a rare breed of truly independent men.

The rest of the journey is less eventful. The slopes are not as fierce, and the snow is turning to slush in some of the valleys. It's becoming almost routine to turn off one glacier onto another, to roar up snowbound mountain passes and see the seals plop back into their ice-holes as we cross the fiords.

We stop for a while at the spot where Patti had an adventure on the way up to Ny Alesund. She lost her way in a 'white-out' and was not found for almost an hour. I hope this isn't an omen for the long journey ahead.

Although we make fast progress towards Longyearbyen, the weather has not finished with us. Turning into the broad valley that leads to the town we are hit full in the face by a blizzard of stinging wet snow and as Heinrich accelerates for home it makes for a hard and uncomfortable end to the ride.

After five and a half hours travelling we see through the murk the first lights of Longyearbyen, and the snowmobiles screech clumsily along the wet highway.

It's half-past ten and we have reached our first town, 812 miles from the North Pole.

1 In the writing, there is a lot of evidence of the type of life that Harald lived. Describe his way of life, giving examples of the evidence available in the passage.

2 The writer uses a variety of detail to give an impression of Harald's character. Show how his character is created through:
 ● physical description;
 ● the account of Harald's relations with the group of travellers;
 ● the account of his possessions;
 ● his attitude to life.

3 How successfully has the writer used language to describe the scene and to create the mood and atmosphere of the place?

4 In your own words explain the meanings of the words and phrases printed below in bold type:

"The second surprise is **how benignly and agreeably** he copes with the appearance of ten tired and hungry travellers in the middle of the night."

"Harald offers advice, comment and information, **liberally laced with dry humour**."

"… but I feel he rather enjoys **being an enigma**."

5 This extract describes one small part of the writer's journey. What are the features in the writing that would make you interested in following the story of the rest of the journey?

Here are a pupil's answers to the comprehension questions. As you are reading them, try to ask yourself these questions, which are about the skills used:
 ● Has he shown understanding of the passage?
 ● Has he been able to select relevant parts of the passage to answer the questions precisely?
 ● Has he supported his answers with adequate evidence, through close reference to examples in the writing?
 ● Does his own written expression help to get across his meanings?

To save you from looking back at the questions on each occasion, these are repeated for you at the start of each answer:

1 In the writing, there is a lot of evidence of the type of life that Harald lived. Describe his way of life, giving examples of the evidence available in the passage.

> 1. Harold lives in an isolated place. He lives an almost solitary existence, only seeing a few people a year. ("Some years I don't see anyone from Autumn to July.") He lives off the food he can hunt from around the mountians and valleys where he lives. As he is further north than the most northern towns he suffers greatly from the cold. He hunts the animals that live in this area; seals, reindeer, salmon, and does quite well from them. As well as living quite a remote and basic life, which is shown because he has no proper toilet and collects his water from the roof of his house, he also has quite a morden furnished home with plenty of comforts,

having things like a remote controlled hi-fi, telephone and large numbers of CD's. He has quite good links to other people. He has his post delivered by a helicopter and he has his phone, but if he had an accident outside the house he probably wouldn't be able to receive any outside assistance.

He has taken advantage of the area he lives in to help equip his home and to help him live. This is shown in the way his wood supply is probably driftwood from the Russian coast and his electricity supply is wind-generated.

Even though Harold's life is one of loneliness, he welcomes visitors with great hospitality. This is shown by the way that he offers good food, Aquavit, and whisky. His way of life is also quite cultured, as he listens to Rachmaninov piano concertos on CD. As well as listening to music, he also seems to have a life where he is a constant reader, perhaps this is to stimulate his mind as he is on his own for the majority of the time.

Examiner's commentary

In this answer the pupil has used a variety of points to show different features of his way of life. Clearly he has gone through the passage and identified the main points. These take account of Harald's surroundings and the way he treats his visitors. Thus, there is good use of the evidence.

2   The writer uses a variety of detail to give an impression of Harald's character. Show how his character is created through:

● physical description;
● the account of Harald's relations with the group of travellers;
● the account of his possessions;
● his attitude to life.

2. When the party reaches Harold's hut it is obvious the author is expecting a very rugged, burly man with a beard, tangled hair and weathered skin. Harold, however, is not the man of the image in the author's mind. He turns out to be "a tall, pale, studious figure." This, plus his rabbi beard, seems to show him to be educated and quite sophisticated.

ANSWERS

His reactions to the appearance of the travellers, in the middle of the night, is genial, with an even temper. They were expecting a stereotype of the local people, rugged and grizzly, but instead he is kind and friendly ("how benignly and agreably he copes with the appearence of ten tired and hungry travellers"). Also, the way he relates to his guests, by listening to and entertaining them, proves him to be an excellent host. Once the party has sat down, to a meal that Harold has prepared, Harold is described as giving "advice, comment and information, liberally laced with dry humour." This might mean that he has a good relationship with the travellers, he can set up an instant friendship, by making himself very popular. But in the way he treats these strangers in his home, it is like he has known them all his life, so he is trusting, and doesn't expect them to do any wrong.

His possessions show him to be a well-educated and modern man with a lot of time to kill. I think although Harold does like and enjoy the outdoors, he also likes the comfort of his own home and he likes some luxuries, but when you think that he possesses up to date facilities like the CDs and the phone, as well as the books, then these may suggest that he is lonely because he cannot relate to or communicate to other people a lot. His attitude to life coupled with his chosen place of residence makes him seem something of a loner, but completely independent and in control of his own life.

Examiner's commentary

Again, the strength of this answer is that the pupil has been methodical. He has treated each section of the question separately and interpreted features of Harald's character from the evidence available.

3 How successfully has the writer used language to describe the scene and to create the mood and atmosphere of the place?

3. I think the writer has been quite successful in his use of description. Much of the description is quite concise, but the adjectives used are in order to help us create a clear picture in our minds, eg "grizzly bearded."

The scene at first seems very primitive, which is shown through description of 'A tall wooden frame hung with seal carcasses,' and the use of the word 'hut' seems in keeping with the archaic scene. This illusion is shattered by the eloquence and humour of the educated dweller's speech.

The atmosphere is one of desolation, portrayed by the picture of "empty mountains" and the way that the helicopter "clatters" into sight. Also, the time of day helps me to create the mood, and then the primitive feeling returns in the description of the toilet and washing facilities, which involve snow, a small bag and a toothbrush. This theme is carried through in a description of the sitting rooms as a "Viking Valhalla" and in the image of Harold as a "warrior slain in battle." This primitive, Northern Viking impression is changed by the presence of the modern conveniences, but the desolation returns when Harold says that some years he sees no-one for six months and that his nearest neighbour lives eighteen miles away. Altogether, the lonely mood is helped by the friendly atmosphere created when Harold has company. One other thing you notice is that it is all written in the present tense, which makes the action feel as if it is happening.

Examiner's commentary

This is a successful answer particularly in the way that the pupil has shown how the atmosphere is created. There are sufficient references to the techniques of language used.

4 In your own words explain the meanings of the words and phrases printed below in bold type:

"The second surprise is how **benignly and agreeably** he copes with the appearance of ten tired and hungry travellers in the middle of the night."

This means that he welcomed the travellers warmly, in a friendly way. He was calm and settling, reassuring towards the ten of them.

"Harald offers advice, comment and information, **liberally laced with dry humour**."

This means that his advice, comments and information always have a bit of wit in them, like a joke to keep the listener interested in what was said.

"… but I feel he rather enjoys **being an enigma**."

> He liked to be a man of contradictions. He kept things secret, and so he was not easy to understand.

Examiner's commentary

The pupil has understood the vocabulary and been able to explain the meanings concisely.

5   This extract describes one small part of the writer's journey. What are the features in the writing that would make you interested in following the story of the rest of the journey?

> 5. I found this passage very interesting and I personally would enjoy reading on. I become interested in the adventures, problems and discoveries that the travellers will make on their journey. I get the impression that if I do read on, the interest will be kept up by the detailed description about his surroundings, and especially about the characters who he comes across. At the end of this extract, I feel that I have got to know Harold, and I predict that there will be many more people who will be described just as well so that I will get to know them just as if I was on the journey too.
>
> Harold's life seems one of repetitiveness: no opportunities crop up each day, few distractions of other humans, very cut off from the outside world. His life will carry on all the time, the door always open as a welcoming sight for all weary travellers passing through his route. I get the feeling that there will be lots more people in other parts of the world and so we will get variety of people in the book. This is what makes me want to read on .

Examiner's commentary

These questions are always difficult because they are so open-ended. This pupil has answered the question well. His reasons for wanting to read on are relevant to the strengths of the passage. He makes points about the qualities of the passage, particularly the way that it deals with understanding of an unusual lifestyle. This is preferable to statements which simply say "I like the passage", or "I would like to read on because it was interesting."

At some point in your GCSE course you will study pre-twentieth century literature; it may be for one of the examination papers or it might be for a piece of coursework.

Printed below is an extract from *Jane Eyre*, a novel which was written in the nineteenth century by Charlotte Brontë.

Read the extract carefully and then consider the question that follows it.

JANE EYRE
by Charlotte Brontë

DURING THESE EIGHT years my life was uniform: but not unhappy, because it was not inactive. I had the means of an excellent education placed within my reach; a fondness for some of my studies, and a desire to excel in all, together with a great delight in pleasing my teachers, especially such as I loved, urged me on: I availed myself fully of the advantages offered me. In time I rose to be the first girl of the first class; then I was invested with the office of a teacher; which I discharged with zeal for two years: but at the end of that time, I altered.

Miss Temple, through all the changes, had thus far continued superintendent of the seminary: to her instruction I owed the best part of my acquirements; her friendship and society had been my continual solace; she stood me in the stead of mother, governess, and, latterly, companion. At this period she married, removed with her husband (a clergyman, and excellent man, almost worthy of such a wife) to a distant county, and consequently was lost to me.

From the day she left I was no longer the same: with her was gone every settled feeling, every association that had made Lowood in some degree a home to me. I had imbibed from her something of her nature and much of her habits: more harmonious thoughts: what seemed better regulated feelings had become the inmates of my mind. I had given in allegiance to duty and order; I was quiet; I believed I was content: to the eyes of others, usually even to my own, I appeared a disciplined and subdued character.

But destiny, in the shape of the Rev Mr Nasmyth, came between me and Miss Temple: I saw her in her travelling dress step in to a post chaise, shortly after the marriage ceremony; I watched the chaise mount the hill and disappear beyond its brow; and then retired to my own room, and there spent in solitude the greatest part of the half-holiday granted in honour of the occasion.

I walked about the chamber most of the time. I imagined myself only to be regretting my loss, and thinking how to repair it; but when my reflections were concluded, and I looked up and found that the afternoon was gone, and evening far advanced, another discovery dawned on me, namely, that in the interval I had undergone a transforming process; that my mind had put off all it had borrowed of Miss Temple – or rather that she had taken with her the serene atmosphere I had been breathing in her vicinity – and that now I was left in my natural element, and beginning to feel the stirring of old emotions. It did not seem as if a prop were withdrawn, but rather as if a motive were gone: it was not the power to be tranquil which had failed me, but the reason for tranquillity was no more. My world had for some years been in Lowood: my experience had been of its rules and systems; now I remembered that the real world was wide, and that a varied field of hopes and fears, of sensations and excitements, awaited those who had courage to go forth into its expanse, to seek real knowledge of life amidst its perils.

I went to my window, opened it and looked out. There were two wings of the building; there was the garden; there were the skirts of Lowood; there was the hilly horizon. My eye passed all other objects to rest on those most remote, the blue peaks: it was those I longed to surmount; all within their boundary of rock and heat seemed prison-ground, exile limits. I traced the white road winding round the base of one mountain, and vanishing in a gorge between the two: how I longed to follow it further! I recalled the time when I had travelled that very road in a coach; I remembered descending that hill at twilight: an age seemed to have elapsed since the day which brought me first to Lowood, and I had never

quitted it since. My vacations had all been spent at school: Mrs Reed had never sent for me to Gateshead; neither she nor any of her family had ever been to visit me. I had no communication by letter or message with the outer world; school rules, school duties, school habits and notions, and voices and faces, and phrases, and costumes, and preferences, and antipathies: such was what I knew of existence. And now I felt that it was not enough: I tired of the routine of eight years in one afternoon. I desired liberty; for liberty I gasped; for liberty I uttered a prayer; it seemed scattered on the wind then faintly blowing. I abandoned it and framed a humbler supplication; for change, stimulus; that petition, too, seemed swept off into vague space: "Then," I cried, half desperate, "grant me at least a new servitude!"

TASK

In this extract Jane is reflecting on her earlier life. What feelings does she convey to you about that early life? You should refer in detail to and use quotations from the extract to illustrate the points you wish to make.

ANSWER

Extract of Jane Eyre.

The first impression I receive from reading through the text, is that the early stage of Jane Eyres life is devoted to the realisation of her own self.

The passage opens by conveying feelings of contentment of security and warmth. These feelings are transmitted to me by the use of strong nouns , 'desire' and 'delight'. As well as the happiness, I feel there is an underlying feeling of restricted urges. 'During these eight years of my life was uniform', this is recognised by Jane but as it is infitting with the way she leads her life this fact remains unchanged.

She is in awe of miss Temple , she feels that it is this remarkable woman that is responsible for all her admirable character traits ' I had imbibed from her something of her nature and much of her habits'. Jane feels happy to have gained these as it is a positive transformation and growth. She believed that she owned the traits and not have had them installed.

The beginning of her discovery starts when her teacher is removed, this instigates the feeling of displacement, her only security and familiarty dispersed. Great sadness and depression follows and this is spurred whilst watching teacher leave as she feels a part of her is leaving too, ' there spent in solitude the greatest part of the half-holiday granted in honor of the occasion'. This period of time is used for reflection, at this point she acknowledges the effect that Miss at this point she acknowledges the effect that Miss Temple had. Her original self begins to return and becomes comfortable - even preferable as the discovery of wide variety of experiences on offer in an unsheltered world. 'a varied field of hopes and fears'. Within her feelings of excitement and anticipation again began to stir. A future filled with knowledge, desperate for adventure a cry for freedom.

Examiner's commentary There are two particular threads to the question that need to be noted. The main thrust of the question requires you to write about Jane's early life and her feelings about it. You should also pay attention to the requirement for quotation and detailed reference.

The answer that is printed above does this quite well. It uses quotation and takes us systematically through the extract analysing as it goes. There is a clear statement in the opening paragraph, "the realisation of her own self". It is Jane's realisation of her own self, most especially on the afternoon of the departure of Miss Temple which is then examined.

There are weaknesses of language and these would have to be taken into account when marking this writing. Attempts to use a wide range of vocabulary occasionally result in rather odd misuse of words. In terms of structure the writing also comes to a rather abrupt end and certainly lacks a full conclusion.

As we have already mentioned, often in English exams you are given a passage of literature or a poem to read and then asked to write in an imaginative way using what you have read as a starting point.

In this case you are going to be given a question which simply asks you to develop a piece of your own writing based on an idea or a theme in the original passage.

You are asked to read an extract from a novel, *A Portrait of the Artist as a Young Man* by James Joyce. This is a well known passage about a young boy receiving a beating at the hands of a cruel teacher. The setting is a religious school in Ireland. The task set at the end of the passage asks you, in a rather general way, to write about an incident involving a teacher and a pupil.

First read the passage, then look at the writing task and consider the options open to you. An example of writing is given.

To set the scene – the Prefect of Studies, Father Dolan, has visited the classroom of Father Arnall. A severe disciplinarian, he has already beaten one boy in the class for doing badly in his Latin grammar. In this passage he turns his attention to Stephen Dedalus, the central character in the story.

> – You, boy, who are you?
> Stephen's heart jumped suddenly.
> – Dedalus, sir.
> – Why are you not writing like the others?
> – I... my...
> He could not speak with fright.
> – Why is he not writing, Father Arnall?
> – He broke his glasses, said Father Arnall, and I exempted him from work.

TWENTIETH CENTURY LITERARY STIMULUS

STIMULUS MATERIAL

– Broke? What is this I hear? What is this your name is? said the prefect of studies.

– Dedalus, sir.

– Out here, Dedalus. Lazy little schemer. I see schemer in your face. Where did you break your glasses?

Stephen stumbled into the middle of the class, blinded by fear and haste.

– Where did you break your glasses? repeated the prefect of studies.

– The cinderpath, sir.

– Hoho! The cinderpath! cried the prefect of studies. I know that trick.

Stephen lifted his eyes in wonder and saw for a moment Father Dolan's whitegrey not young face, his baldy whitegrey head with fluff at the sides of it, the steel rims of his spectacles and his nocoloured eyes looking through the glasses. Why did he say he knew that trick?

– Lazy idle little loafer! cried the prefect of studies. Broke my glasses! An old schoolboy trick. Out with your hand this moment!

Stephen closed his eyes and held out in the air his trembling hand with the palm upwards. He felt the prefect of studies touch it for a moment at the fingers to straighten it and then the swish of the sleeve of the soutane as the pandybat was lifted to strike. A hot burning stinging tingling blow like the loud crack of a broken stick made his trembling hand crumple together like a leaf in the fire; and at the sound and the pain scalding tears were driven into his eyes. His whole body was shaking with fright, his arm was shaking and his crumpled burning livid hand shook like a loose leaf in the air. A cry sprang to his lips, a prayer to be let off. But though the tears scalded his eyes and his limbs quivered with pain and fright he held back the hot tears and the cry that scalded his throat.

– Other hand! shouted the prefect of studies.

(N.B. James Joyce was a writer who experimented with his writing by not using speech marks for direct speech. You are advised to use speech marks in your writing. You can remind yourself of the use of speech marks by consulting p8.)

TASK Write about an incident involving a teacher and a pupil.

> **Examiner's tip**   Notice, as in this case here, that you are often not given very precise instructions for an imaginative writing task. One of the skills you must use is to interpret the question and see if you can think of an original idea. You are sometimes given some extra guidance which, in this case might be as follows:
>
> "You could write about an imagined event as part of a story or, if you prefer, you could write about a real event."
>
> How can you help yourself to make a decision about what to write? Firstly, check that you have clearly understood the wording in the task. Here, "Write about an incident involving a teacher and a pupil" gives you a wide choice. You are certainly not restricted to writing about a school teacher and school pupil – there are literally hundreds of other possibilities, and you might please an examiner by coming up with an original idea!
>
> Read the example of writing in response to this task. You will see that this pupil appears not to use the story as a starting point at all. His writing suggests that he has interpreted the task very differently. However, if you look closely at his plan, you can begin to see links. He has in fact used a theme of physical punishment and turned it into a very different sort of story.
>
> Before reading it though, let us think about how it might have been planned.

PLANNING

What is involved in planning?

Planning can give you an initial idea; it can provide you with a shape or structure to your writing and it can allow you to think about possible scenes for description.

You will know what sorts of plans you feel comfortable with. Some students prefer to plan in a diagram, such as a spider diagram. Others prefer to write lists of events and ideas. Or you can "think aloud" with your writing – quickly jotting down all the ideas as they occur to you.

What is the link between a plan and the writing?

The purpose of a good plan is not to give you every idea or every word of your work! It is more to start you off and give you confidence. Think of it like a skeleton; your writing can then put all the flesh onto the bones.

One word of warning! Do not become a slave to the plan. Change your ideas as you see new possibilities, whilst you are writing. Here are three types of plan which could be used for the writing on pp36–7:

1 DIAGRAMMATIC

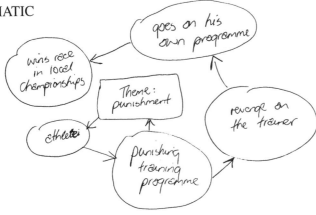

2 A LIST

- punishment
- theme of punishment in athletics
- boy being trained by cruel trainer
- revenge against trainer
- wins competition

3 "THINKING ALOUD"

I can see a boy who is an athlete and he is being overtrained by a harsh trainer who because he was injured wants the boy to win but he really wants to win for himself – the boy rejects the trainer and trains himself – this leads to an ending where the boy wins, the trainer sees this at the championships

ANSWER

<u>"Write Imaginatively about an incident involving a teacher and a pupil."</u>

"Run faster, boy! You're not trying," bellowed Mr. Graham.

Mark was running 1500m in his twice-weekly lunchtime training session for the forthcoming regional Junior Athletics Championship. Mr. Graham had agreed to take him on and train him. A tall, powerfully built former athlete, Mr. Graham never seemed satisfied with any of his pupils' achievements. His own athletic career had sadly been cut short when he badly broke his leg falling down some steps. As a result of this he now walked with a kind of sideways limp that made him look like he was not totally balanced all of the time.

"Come on Mark, you're not putting in any effort! Don't you want me to enter you for the Junior Athletics Championship?"

Mark crossed the finish line and sat down, exhausted on the rubber track.

"I was trying, sir. It's my ankle, sir. It's gone all stiff," complained Mark between breaths. He thought this injury was probably because of Mr. Graham's insistence that he ran 1500 metres at least six times a week.

"Get back onto the track, Mark. You'll only get better with practice," Mr. Graham was a great believer in those old sayings.

"Can't I have a break please? I've been running all lunchtime. Surely I'm fast enough to enter the Championship now!" Mark knew that his time was around the level needed for entry, but to win he needed something extra.

"I give up! You just do not have the right attitude for athletics. You can enter the championship if you like, but I'm not training you anymore! You should know by now that pride comes before a fall."
or before?!

Mr. Graham walked off as briskly as his ankle would allow, leaving Mark sitting on the track, his head in his hands.

Mark vowed to himself that he would enter the Junior Athletic championship and he would win the 1500 metres, just to show Mr. Graham that he was wrong to not believe in his ability. He told himself that he would design a training schedule that he felt happy with. He would make use of the two weeks before the Championship to maximise his potential.

He had decided that varying the type of running would be more likely to improve his chances of winning than the intensive 1500 metre work demanded of him by Mr. Graham. He sent off the entry form for the championship by first class post and waited anxiously for the reply to be sent back, showing if he had fulfilled the entry requirements. This came back satisfactorily and the rest of the two weeks passed very quickly.

On the morning of the Championship, Mark was up early to perform his stretching exercises. His father drove him to the nearby athletics ground. He warmed up, then his first heat was called onto the track. Mark walked out nervously, worried whether going it alone was the right decision, after all, Mr. Graham was an ex-athlete himself. If Mark did not win this heat, he could not get into the final, and Mr. Graham would have achieved victory over him.

The race was actually just a formality. Mark won by ten seconds, so went on to the semi-final. This time, though, he was not so lucky. Three of the racers crossed the line at the same time. The result had to go to the judges for adjudication. While Mark was waiting, he saw an old car pull up and a man limp out to join the crowd. Mark's name rang out over the public address system in the list of finalists. Mr. Graham presented him with the gold certificate.

Examiner's commentary

This pupil has achieved a strong sense of character, for both the athlete and the trainer. This has been achieved through the use of dialogue which is used mainly to define the characters. Also, attention is paid to the key relationship between the two characters.

There is considerable variety in the way that the writing is structured. As readers we move from the dialogue during the training session, to a glimpse of Mr Graham's past, when we learn about his accident, then the point where Mark ("that evening") sends off his entry form for the championships, and finally we are brought to the day of the championships when Mr Graham comes back into the story. In fact, the plot is organised in such a way that the reader follows the experiences of the main character to the point where his problems are resolved by a deliberately constructed ending.

There is a good effort to achieve a number of themes in the writing: the punishment in the training schedule at the start; the over zealous enthusiasm of Mr Graham, in the hope that his pupil can be triumphant in his place; and then the themes of rejection, perseverance and triumph towards the end.

There is variety in the sentence structure, much of which is complex. This is an important skill – the ability to write in sentences which cover a number of points through linked or contrasting phrases. There is correct use of tenses in the use of verbs, and a number of effective adjectives and adverbs are also used. The punctuation and paragraphing, two other key skills, are also accurate.

Above all, the pupil is clearly in control of his ideas here and this gives the story a sense of progression. This may have been the result of careful planning.

MEDIA STIMULUS

The next two pages contain an example of stimulus material taken from a media source: a newspaper article. Think about how the style of writing, and the vocabulary, differs from the stimulus material taken from literature.

STIMULUS MATERIAL

Care? We don't even want to know

Contact with a mentally handicapped man teaches Brian Jenkins something about society's – and his own – prejudices

People always try to ignore David. This is a pity because David is one of the friendliest people around. Most days he commutes by train, and he always tries to talk to other passengers; but they usually ignore him. Apart from being so friendly, what makes David different from other commuters is that he is mentally handicapped.

When I first saw David (not his real name), I put him down as someone to be avoided. But it was not easy. Every morning there he would be, chatting to whomever was around, shouting greetings to the platform staff and waving to the train drivers.

Most people he spoke to quickly acknowledged him, and walked on. Everyone else, including me, steered clear. Then one day he caught me unawares. I was reading when I heard a voice close by: 'Hello'. I looked up and there he was, grinning widely.

'Oh, hello,' I mumbled, forcing a smile, and turned back to my book. He said something I could not understand. 'Pardon?' I replied. He repeated it; again I could not make it out. Not wishing to appear rude, I replied, 'Oh, really?'. I tried to look engrossed in my book and wished he would go away. He did not. Instead he became my regular travelling companion.

Every morning I shared half an hour on the train with him and while I never found out much about him, I learned a bit about myself and my prejudices, and something about our society.

David must be in his late forties, he is just under 6ft and quite stocky. He has difficulty walking and shuffles his feet. His short-cut hair is grey. He is always smiling, and there is nearly always a drip on the end of his nose. His clothes seem to fit badly, his trousers sag and his blue jacket is a little small.

He always sports a few railway badges and carries a shoulder bag that contains his notebook and packed lunch. When he reaches his destination for the day, he will stand on the platform, noting down the numbers of passing trains, and later will noisily eat his cling-film-wrapped white-bread sandwiches.

Every day he would shout his greeting across the crowded platform. I felt everyone's eyes on me. They seemed glad it was me, not them. Sometimes I heard comments like, 'It's all right, that man must be looking after him' or, 'They really shouldn't let these people out.'

A few years ago Jasper Carrot exposed our fear of mentally handicapped people when he asked 'Why does the looney on the bus always sit next to me?' By laughing, we shared the feeling. As I spent more time with David, I wanted to find out about him. But anything other than questions such as where had he been and where was he going were met with a blank smile. Once I told him I had seen a very unusual train. He asked me if he was going to see it. I replied that there was no way I could know, but he asked me again and again if he was going to see it.

I believe David lives with his family, and I presume they pay for his travels. As he is out and about almost everyday, and occasionally he goes further afield for a few days, his fares must cost quite a bit, even with his Disabled Person's Railcard. Perhaps he had an accident that left him like this, and he is living off the damages or a pension.

One day he showed me some photographs, mainly of trains, stations and gardens. One picture was of an elderly woman. 'Who's this?' I asked. 'My mum,' he replied indignantly, as if I should already know. There was another one of him and a young woman. They were standing under a tree. She looked friendly and kindly. He had his arm round her. 'That's my girlfriend,' he said.

Some time later I met him the day after his

birthday, and he told me about the presents and cards he had received. But, he added sadly, he had not received one from his girlfriend. This was the first time I ever noticed his smile fade.

There was a time when I found myself almost envying David. He did not have to worry about his job, his mortgage, or the rust on his car. He spent every day doing what he liked, train spotting. I thought there was something endearing about this adult with a child's outlook. Then, when I caught him off guard, I saw he looked sad and lost. And I remembered that children have sadness and frustration as much, if not more than, adults.

After some weeks of commuting together, I started to tire of his company. The difficult conversations that led nowhere were hard work. David did not respond to the usual polite signals. I was trying to tell him that I did not want his company, but he did not understand.

I had to face up to a dilemma. Should I treat him as an equal and explain that I needed to be left alone, or should I make a special allowance? The one thing I did not want was to hurt his feelings. In the end I decided to do what I wanted: I explained that I needed to work on the train, and asked if he would allow me to get on with it.

It did not work. In the end I would avoid him at the station. I would duck behind pillars or lurk at the end of the platform. But sometimes he would still see me, and would rub my nose in my guilt by coming over, full of smiles, to say hello. Occasionally he would offer me a Mars Bar, or ask if I wanted a coffee.

Then I changed my commuting pattern, and I no longer caught the same train as David. In a strange way I missed his company. For months I did not see him, then one day, out of the train window, I saw him on the platform. There he was smiling away, talking to a woman. She obviously was not enjoying his company.

I realised how awful we are: David is seriously disadvantaged, and yet all he wants from the rest of us is a bit of friendship. It made me see how the concept of 'Care in the Community' was flawed. As a community, we just do not care, we do not even want to know. And that is probably our loss.

1 From the article, state four facts about David.

2 Identify and comment on four things that can be understood about David from the passage.

3 Write about ways in which the writer uses language to express his views.

4 What meanings and ideas are there in the final two sentences of the article?

5 Write a brief article of your own persuading teenagers to treat disabled people sympathetically.

TASK

Examiner's tip Here you are asked to show that you can tell the difference between facts and ideas, or inferences. The reading skills that are tested are the selection of information, and then commenting, or evaluating how that information is used. In question 4 you are also being asked to make effective use of information in your own writing.

A close reading of the passage is important. Then, in question 1 you will need to identify clearly what can be stated as fact. Question 2 explores points that can be more widely understood – points that can be inferred, implied in the writing, in other words, points that can be "picked up" through a close reading. Question 3 is another of those questions which asks you to comment on the use of language. You really ought to consider the way that there is a mixture of personal story and argument, designed to enlist our sympathy, and perhaps our feelings of guilt. Question 4 asks for understanding of a particularly important part of the passage, and finally, question 5 tests both reading and writing skills. You will need to use the ideas in your own writing, and to make sure that you are writing for a purpose – here, to explain and persuade.

In the following answer, the examiner recognises that many of the skills have been covered successfully, although in the first question, bald facts are not really stated with absolute confidence.

<u>Care ? We don't even want to know.</u>   5.12.96   i.

1. 4 significant facts about David.

i. David is unaware that people try to avoid him, he goes to them and tries to make friends, but all the time, he is naive to the fact that they don't want to talk to him.

ii. David has quite a lot of confidence. it takes a lot of 'guts' to approach a stranger and try to start a friendly conversation.

iii. David has some secret sorrow, that he momentarily is reminded of, and a pained look crosses his face.

iv. He is childlike in his approach to life He seems to have endless enthusiasm for life, but like many children (and adults) he has moments of sadness.

   <u>Are these all straight facts?</u>

2. Identify and comment on four points that can be inferred from the passage, about David.

i. "Most people he spoke to quickly acknowledged him, and walked on
- This shows that David is thought of as a nuisance. People try to avoid him, and try to get out of a lengthy conversation with him. They find him strange, and abnormal, so therefore he must be avoided. People's views, towards David are very naive and prejudiced, they don't understand what motivates him, so therefore he must be weird.

ii. "Should I treat him as an equal and explain that I needed to be left alone, or should I make a special allowance?"
- When a person of normal mentality starts a friendly conversation up with you on the train, you reply and speak about neutral topics. But because David is mentally handicapped, they feel that he is unable to keep up a friendly conversation, and that he may take advantage of a situation, and maybe very volatile. But no one is willing to give him that chance. Do you really have too much work to do on the train, or is that just an excuse to get rid of him. Surely he should be given a chance, and treated as an equal, to prove himself,

and to let him speak to you, to make a new friend, which would obviously please him.

iii. "I never found out much about him, I learned a bit about myself and my prejudices, and something about our society
- This is a very thoughtful sentence. It shows how people can be prejudiced, without even realising that they are. To generalise about society as a whole, shows the way that a mentally handicapped person's persistence, can open your eyes to the whole naivity of society today. David is like a normal happy go lucky child, and that he is harmless. When he wishes to speak with you, he does it purely for companionship and probably is not intelligent enough for any harmful ulterior motive, that the public expect him to have.

iv. "There was a time when I found myself almost enjoying David."

-This statement seems to me to be very hurtful. David is happy with his life and knows no different. I think that it is wrong to envy someone because they have no responsibilities. Although I'm sure he wouldn't want your pity, David will never experience the joys of some parts of adult life, he is stuck in a time warp. I'm sure that if David understood, he would rather be mentally normal, and have bills etc, than be a child all his life. ✓

3. The language that the author uses to express his views, see to be fairly basic, aimed at an audience of all ages, with fairly basic language and a sophisticated layout of his views, opinions and narrative.

There is a certain amount of guilt voiced through the writer, making you feel ashamed of any prejudices you, as the reader, have ever had, and are likely to have, in a similar situation.

Brian Jenkins lays out his thoughts in a very orderly way. Going from annoyance, to guilt, to annoyance and then to guilt, sympathy and a slight amount of pity.

The writer uses fairly detailed descriptions of situations, but he shows that the outcome is always the same. He always gets to the point fairly quickly. Brian Jenkins tries to generalise, to get to the point of all prejudices across society. He tries to broaden people's minds, to show that almost everybody has prejudices about something and/or someone. Brian Jenkins tries to get us to acknowledge our prejudices and work through them.

As Brian Jenkins writes about a true story, the way he comes to the point about general prejudices is not condascending or patronising, which through his narrative, helps us to come to terms with any adverse thoughts that we may have. Good, effective analysis.

4. 'As a community, we just do not care, we do not even want to know. And that is probably our loss'

-Brian Jenkins describes many prejudices generally. It is our loss if we don't help people at a disadvantage, as we have help we can give them, but there is probably a lot that they could give you. People think of helping disabled people as a one way thing, we do all the giving, whilst the disabled people do all the taking. But the other people, the disabled people, also have a lot to give. They can open your eyes to many issues and problems that they have. Many mentally handicapped people are have naive to many troubles, and so are therefore calm, and at peace with the world and themselves. These people, may be able to help you relax, as the helper, just by conveying their tranquility to you.

Interesting thoughts here.

41

5. Write an article for a teenage magazine persuading young people to treat mentally handicapped people sympathetically.

In your eyes they are strange and weird. But to themselves they are content children. When you look at a mentally handicapped person, they may look perfectly normal, if any human is "normal". Until they speak or even move, they are just like you or me. But when it dawns on you, that they are infact different, you put up a wall between you and the mentally handicapped person. Why?

Unless you are used to people with a mental handicap, I'm sure most would do it. But these people are just niave and young, in mind, even if not in body. Sure, some mentally handicapped people are crazed murderers or have suicidal tendancies, but not the majority.

Many with mental hanicaps just want friendship and will be content with that. But others want more - taking to the park or to the cinema, by you. Special care workers can do that but do they have time to sit, and listen, and be a real freind. You could do that.

Even giving a friendly smile to a person with disabilities or walking by and saying 'hi', to a person you see regularly. Why not ?, it doesn't cost you anything. But as many of them are young in the mind, they will be able to return the smile or hi, but not able to give you the real knowledge that they want more than hi, so they will be content with that.

When passing a mentally handicapped person, don't give them a wide berth, point and laugh at them, don't intentionally or even unintentionally hurt their feelings. Walk by, don't stare, even give them a smile, and make their day.

Treat them as one of you, because they are. Treat them, as you would expect others to treat you. You wouldn't want people to stare, point or make fun of you, so why do it to them? Treat them as a friend, not as an enemy.

They are the ones that have to live with the problem of being mentally handicapped, not you. Make their lives easier, not harder.

Excellent — good range of understanding: points well made, and a persuasive article of your own.

(A)

One of the types of non-fiction writing specified in the National Curriculum is travel writing.

Printed below is an extract from the Summer 1995 *AA Magazine* in which a particular drive in the Lake District of northern England is described. Read the passage carefully and then consider the questions which follow it.

AA Great Drives: Vroom! with a view

Are there any 'great drives' left to be had in this country? Can you still climb in the car and escape to another, better world? The answer, if I hadn't known it before, was yes; here was the proof – a breathtaking view of England's last wilderness.

I was 1,940 windswept feet above sea level, on the western flank of the Pennines, halfway through a 180 mile drive suggested by the *AA Tour Guide Britain*: the view was a bonus, because the drive up from Melmerby to Hartside Top had in itself been five miles of pure motoring pleasure. And then it was a memorable run over the high moors to the little town of Alston.

The route up the A686 through the Cumbrian hills was one of the highlights of my tour. I'd set off from Carlisle, which is marking the 250th anniversary of its role in Bonnie Prince Charlie's ill-fated rebellion. If you're travelling *en famille*, the children could discover the more blood-curdling aspects of feuding at medieval Carlisle Castle, which fell to the Scots in 1745. It lies within musket range of the B5299 that runs through gentle meadows with the Lake District's peak spanning the southern horizon.

There are splendid views across the glistening Solway Firth to Scotland from a point just before the road dips into Caldbeck. The village churchyard is home to the grave of John Peel, the 19th-century huntsman famed in song.

Wandering sheep are typical moorland hazards on the unclassified road that winds towards Bassenthwaite Lake – a great finger of water that beckons you into the heart of the Lake District. This is where the really spectacular scenery and demanding contours begin, so the car has to work that much harder.

The Winlatter Pass climbs through a pine forest, then runs down to the pleasant village of Low Lorton. A few miles later, the B5289 wriggles along the virtually uninhabited shores of Crummock Water and Buttermere, two of the region's smallest and most beautiful lakes (could it be time for a picnic?).

The road appears to be heading for a cul-de-sac, hemmed in by craggy mountains streaked by waterfalls. But it swings left and climbs the dramatic Honister Pass, snaking between steep, scree-covered slopes littered with huge boulders. Once a year, the quarry at the top of the Pass is the venue for the Vintage Sports Car Club's idiosyncratic Lakeland Trial. Bugattis, Bentleys and other valuable old-timers attempt to climb a long, rough, slippery twisting track that ordinary mortals would think twice about tackling in a modern four-wheel-drive Land Rover.

On the far side of the Pass, the B5289 ducks and dives through wooded Borrowdale before entering Keswick. The busy little

town, once a market and mining centre, is now a magnet for tourists, walkers and climbers. I headed for the Cars of the Stars Motor Museum, run by a local dentist, where the attractions include two batmobiles, Patrick McGoohan's Lotus Super Seven from *The Prisoner*, the Aston Martin driven by James Bond and the reliant Regal van run by Derek 'Del Boy' Trotter in BBC-TV's *Only Fools and Horses*. And if that doesn't grab the children, there's the world's largest pencil at the Cumberland Pencil Museum. Coloured pencils have been manufactured in Keswick since the mid-19th century and originally depended on the local graphite deposit.

Helvellyn's pine-clad slopes shelter the A 591 as it sweeps down to Grasmere. This Lakeland landscape was muse to Wordsworth who lived in Dove Cottage in Grasmere and at Rydal Mount down the road. At the entrance to Grasmere churchyard, where the poet is buried, what used to be the

village school is now a tiny shop. I left with several pieces of the local gingerbread, made to a secret recipe since Queen Victoria was on the throne.

Maximum concentration is essential on the A593 from Ambleside to Coniston. Despite its A-class status, this is a narrow road that, in places, winds between intimidating stone walls. Coniston's forested hinterland offers fine walks; if you seek a more sedate pace, take a cruise aboard *Gondola*, a 136-year-old steam yacht restored by the National Trust. She glides along Coniston Water, where Donald Campbell's attempt on the world water speed record ended in tragedy in 1967. His jet-powered *Bluebird* was doing about 300mph when it crashed.

Coniston is also a good place for an overnight stop. I can endorse the AA's opinion of the Premier Selected 17th-century Wheelgate Country House Hotel. Run by Joan and Roger Lupton, this hideaway offers a warm welcome
– from a

Hawkshead and Near Sawrey, where Beatrix Potter lived at Hill Top, a 17th-century farmhouse. The world of Peter Rabbit and other Potter creations is brought to life in the drawings at the museums here – a possible diversion for little children. But I drove on, somewhat concerned that the Wheelgate Hotel's generous breakfast would exceed the eight-ton weight limit for the ferry, which takes four minutes to reach Bowness-on-Windermere. The Steamboat Museum nearby features working vintage craft.

North of Windermere, fields bright with buttercups flank the A592 as it starts its long and increasingly spectacular charge to the Kirkstone Pass. This serpentine road requires the driver to concentrate on the car's ride, roadholding, steering, brakes, acceleration and gearbox. It also measures a driver's patience if stuck behind a coach, because overtaking opportunities are as rare as snowmen in the Sahara.

The mood changes while driving along the western shore of Ullswater. You pass the Aira force waterfall, the place where Wordsworth was inspired by 'a host of golden daffodils', and gradually exchange the Lake District's craggy grandeur for softer landscapes near Penrith. A mile or two of dual-carriageway spans the M6, then it's on to the

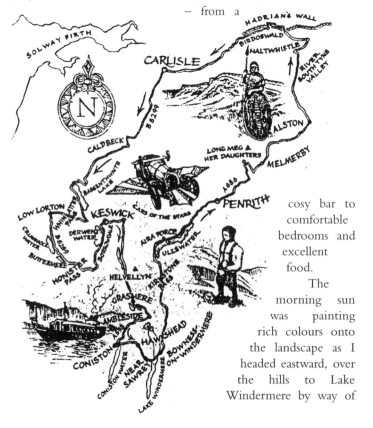

cosy bar to comfortable bedrooms and excellent food.

The morning sun was painting rich colours onto the landscape as I headed eastward, over the hills to Lake Windermere by way of

A686 and you come upon the lovely Eden valley.

If you want to share a Cumbrian secret, turn left for Hunsonby, about 1.5 miles after Langwathby and follow the lanes to where Long Meg and her Daughters stand in a field in an isolated farm. Few discover this prehistoric stone circle – and the absence of visitors makes it all the more magical. It's only a five-mile detour.

Stop for a coffee and delicious home-made goodies at the Village Bakery in Melmerby; then it's a pleasant 10-mile drive to Alston, which is England's highest town. This is where the mood changes again as moorland gives way to the valley of the South Tyne river.

The last six miles of the drive to Haltwhistle are a delight, because this is a road whose quality belies its unclassified status.

Today's motorists can cover in a few effortless minutes distances that represented a brutally long day's march to the legionnaires who manned Hadrian's Wall, north of Haltwhistle. The Roman Army Museum at Greenhead is a tribute to them. Nearby, the other tangible links with Roman times include the fort at Birdoswald, where the road runs past a well-preserved length of the coast-to-coast wall that protected the Roman Empire's northern frontier.

Later, on the road back to Carlisle, I found myself reflecting that there are two equally rewarding aspects to a great drive. For some the pleasure of motoring lies in the freedom to stop and to savour the scenery. For others, the quality of driving is the paramount consideration. Take this heart of Lakeland drive and both wishes will be delightfully fulfilled.

1 The writer of this article describes what he is writing about as a "great drive". In no more than 150 words summarise why he considers it to be a "great drive". Then briefly give your opinion of what he says.

2 The article is set out in a way which is designed to attract you to the idea of doing the trip yourself. Analyse the way in which the article is written and the way in which it was presented. Does it succeed in its aim?

You should refer to: the vocabulary and writing style

the layout and use of illustration.

TASK

Examiner's tip The key to success in answering this question is to identify the skills that you are being asked to use. Try to use each skill as precisely as possible. In Question 1 you are asked first of all to write a summary. Here, it is important to stick to the limit of 150 words. Be clear about each separate point – summary is a precise exercise and you cannot include anything other than the key points. The second part of Question 1 is more open, involving the skill of evaluation. When you are asked to give your opinion on the writer's views, make sure that what you write is i) genuinely based on what the the writer has said; ii) of significance; iii) supported by argument or evidence. Note that you are not simply being asked to give your opinion on the topic; you are asked to respond to the *writer's* views.

The second question requires a close analysis of language. This is an important question as it tests your understanding of how language is used for particular purposes and effects. You would be expected to comment on some of the persuasive, descriptive style of language, which has an effect of a relaxed, easy approach relevant to a leisurely drive or holiday mood. In addition, there are aspects of the graphics and structure that, you might decide, help the reader to follow the points, such as the columns, the illustrations and the use of maps.

Don't forget that you are also asked to evaluate the language. Does it succeed? This requires more than a yes or no answer! You must be prepared to provide reasons and support these with evidence from the article.

Letts

Q&A

ANSWER

Travel Writing

The route passes through England's last wilderness which includes gentle meadows, pine forests, beautiful lakes, a waterfall and numerous picturesque villages. This breathtaking scenery all adds to why he finds the drive so appealing.

His second and most detailed reason is that there are so many interesting places to visit. The area has a number of museums ranging from famous cars to the Roman army museum. The journey also takes in the grave of John Peel, Carlisle Castle, the home of Beatrix Potter and a prehistoric stone circle.

His final reason as to why this is a 'great drive' is the pure driving pleasure that can be gained from the narrow, winding roads. The encompassing stone walls add a touch of danger to the drive which cause the driver to concentrate on his steering, braking, accelerating and gear changing, all the things that make driving so enjoyable.

I think that that the writer has to say is quite interesting and very well expressed. He uses a lot of detail during his exploration of the local sights, which along with his inclusion of historical references provides a lot of interesting information about the area. This makes the area seem more appealing to the reader. I especially like what he has to say about the views and driving. He uses an excellent selection of adjectives, such as 'splendid' and 'spectacular' to describe the quite breathtaking views. His description of the driving conditions and driving itself is brilliant, especially the way he describes the roads as 'serpentine' and states that 'the car has to work that much harder, which really highlights the thrills that can be obtained from driving on the winding roads.

The article is written in an informal and very informative style. The writer uses a lot of information when referring to the different sights and places to visit on the trip. Not only does the writer use a lot of information to describe the sights, such as including the main attractions at the cars at the sports motor museum, but he gives a little historical insight into the place. Things like mentioning Donald Campbell's death on the Coniston water, whilst attempting to break the world water speed record, make the locations seem more interesting.. This in turn will entice more people into doing the drive.

The use of vocabulary is also impressive as it helps to bring across the real beauty of the area which is one of the article's main features in terms of attracting drivers. The use of adjectives like 'breathtaking' and 'spectacular' when describing the views, tells you that the views are obviously extremely beautiful but without saying just what they are. This leaves a touch of intrigue and curiosity in the mind of the reader which again will help to attract drivers. The vocabulary used to describe the actual driving is very clever. 'This is where the really spectacular scenery and demanding contours begin, so the car has to work that much harder,' is a brilliant use of vocabulary as the use of the adjective 'demanding' makes the driving seem that little bit more challenging which would definitely appeal to any driving enthusiasts who were considering doing the drive.

The use of illustrations in the article is a very successful way of showing the beauty of the area. The pictures are well set out so that they catch the eye and are quite logical as they are positioned next to the relevant text. The pictures show a mixture of the countryside and activities in the area so that they back up the text with a visual presentation. The best use of illustrations is the map of the area. It is very informative and unlike most maps is interesting and visually stunning as the use of diagrams is a clever way of showing where the activities are.

The article most certainly succeeds in its aim to encourage people to do the trip. By describing the picturesque landscape, the numerous places to visit and the driving pleasure that can be obtained from the trip, it appeals to a wide variety of people and makes the trip sound very interesting and most importantly, very inviting.

What follows are two pieces of stimulus material, one from a media source and one from a non-fiction source, an autobiography. Both pieces appeared in The Sunday Times 15 October 1995. The task gives you the chance to practise three different types of response.

Read both passages carefully.

A GENTLE TOUCH FOR THE PUPILS SICK OF SCHOOL

With the initial excitement of starting at the "big" school behind them, the vast majority of Year 7 pupils at comprehensives have settled comfortably into a new routine. But for others the transition is a cause of considerable distress.

It is believed that up to 140,000 children in Britain could be suffering from "school phobia" and a big "trigger point" is the change of schools at 11. The emotional wrench caused by exchanging the comparative security of a small primary school for the perceived impersonality of a large comprehensive can cause a phobia to take route. Phobic symptoms include bed-wetting, headaches and being physically sick at the mere thought of school. Other warning signs are excessive worrying about uniform, using the toilet, changing for PE and eating in public. As the phobia grows, the child will often give up social activities such as sports or Scouts in order to avoid any contact whatsoever with other children.

What can be done? Already comprehensives are eager to build friendly links with their feeder primary schools and comprehensive teachers are regular visitors to primary school assemblies. All comprehensives are now keen to foster a pupil-friendly image and glossy prospectuses are distributed showing the "fun" side of school life. "Taster" days are set up when Year 6 children can meet their new teachers and get used to finding their way around their future school.

John Deacon, head of Poltair school in St Austell, Cornwall, believes that this is not enough. Taking pupils from 22 feeder schools, some with as few as 80 on the roll, there is the obvious risk that a new pupil will feel lost in the 1200 strong comprehensive. To combat this Deacon has set up a carefully planned familiarisation programme. Children from Year 7 in the comprehensive school return to their former schools to work on dance and drama projects and the primary school children spend whole days at the comprehensive. Rather than simply receiving sample lessons, the children mix with those from the year above them and participate fully in classwork. They gain reassurance from talking with the older children and, as a result, few experience a sense of trauma when they move up.

Of course, for some the culture shock of the comprehensive is still hard to assimilate. If problems do arise then, again, the emphasis is placed on the child receiving help from fellow pupils. Deacon sees this as the key to his school's success in helping new pupils to find their feet.

"Children with problems are very unlikely to share their worries with a teacher, so we provide them with 'mentors' – children a year older who help them cope with the practicalities and who try to find out what is really bothering them," he said. "Things like the lunchtime eating arrangements can be a cause of concern and the mentor helps the child through these potentially worrying points in the school day. The mentor reports back to the head of year and often something trivial is the cause of the anxiety. Hopefully, the head of year can reassure the pupil and the problem can be nipped in the bud."

THE RELUCTANT BOARDER

… We were the first to arrive, a habit my mother never lost, much to the amusement of the other kids at school. Nobody else arrived for about three hours. We were greeted by Brother Bede, a tall ginger-bearded Geordie, who was dressed from head to toe in a black robe, finished off with a white dog collar. I remember my mother taking me up to my dormitory, making my bed and unpacking my stuff into the tatty wooden locker beside it. I was to share a room with 11 other boys. I remember needing to go to the lavatory and being confused by the wall of urinals – I had never seen any before. I don't remember much about the other children, who arrived throughout the afternoon, but my mother tells me I was shy and a bit nervous of them. They were all much older than me: I was the youngest by two years. The only friend I made initially was Sausage, the school cat, a fat tabby whose eventual fate defies description.

At about 4.00 p.m. it was time to say goodbye to my mother. It must have been so much harder for her, because she knew what was happening. She said: "I have to go Stephane." I calmly acknowledged this fact and kissed her on the cheek. I then turned to Brother Bede and said: "I would like to be called Steve from now on." God knows why I did it, but my mother instantly said: "No, your name is Stephane and I want you to be called Stephane." Brother Bede agreed and I didn't push the issue any further. My mother left in her car, drove 100 metres up the road and burst into tears. I carried on playing happily with Sausage the cat.

It wasn't until bedtime that the whole thing really began to dawn on me. I couldn't understand why I was going to bed in this strange place and why my mother still hadn't come to pick me up. I had shared a bed with my mother since I was a baby. I remember getting out of bed and hearing others around me whimpering in the darkness. I strode out of the dormitory into the hall, half expecting my mother to be there. She wasn't. I walked along the hall and turned right into the refectory. I called out for her. No answer. I started to feel anxious and began to cry. I returned to the hall and in the distance I could just make out the outline of a figure approaching. I called out again, thinking it must be her. No answer. The figure drew nearer. It was Brother Bede. "What are you doing out of bed?" he asked. "I was looking for my mum," I replied, between snuffles. He then went on to explain everything that my mother had already told me and that, basically, I was not going to see her for some time.

1 Read the first passage again carefully and summarise the problems which young children might have when they start a new school.

2 The writer of the autobiography wants us to have sympathy with him as a young boy. Explain how he has written in a way which engages our sympathy. You may refer to:

• the vocabulary he has used;

• the lengths of sentences and phrases;

• the detail of the events which are described.

3 Imagine that you are Stephane. You have been at your boarding school for half a term. Write a letter home to your mother telling her about your life.

In the summary, a word limit is not stated. It is still important that the main points are summarised as precisely as possible. This is the sort of exercise which tests your understanding of key points in a passage, and your ability to rewrite them as clearly as you can. Make sure that you do not write too much.

Question 2 requires an analysis of the language in the autobiography. You have to ask yourself: what is the writer doing with language in order to make an impact on me? Whenever you are asked to comment on how a writer has written, you are inevitably being asked to talk about language.

In Question 3 you will need to take on the role of the character and write in an appropriate tone. This is an imaginative task and so it will be a good idea to think out some ideas first: What kinds of things might he write about? What sorts of events might have happened? Will the life at the school have changed during half a term? Obviously, it is a personal letter, so the tone will be informal, but that should not stop you from including details about the life of the school, some of which you can pick up in the extract.

ANSWER

When children start a new school it can sometimes be very problematic. Occasionally they may be so distressed and disconcerted that they may be suffering from 'school phobia.' This is when a child is so nervous and upset about joining their new school that they begin to wet the bed, receive pounding headaches and are actually being not only mentally ill but physically thick at even just the thought of going to school. This usually occurs when 11 year old children begin their secondary school education.

The children may feel a great sense of insecurity as they have transferred from a known primary school atmosphere to an alien secondary school atmosphere. The fear that this can inflict can be quite unbelievable, but for many of these children it is very significant. Other problems that the children may face are feeling the trauma and loss in a large secondary school especially if they're finding the culture shock difficult to come to terms with, but also they may begin to worry about trivial things such as their uniform and the way it looks; using the toilet facilities; eating whilst other people are watching, especially if the child is on their own; and changing for PE, if they are insecure about their looks or just changing with other people.

If phobias are allowed to grow then they will gradually destroy and self confidence or self belief that the child possessed. It may end up to the extent where the child cuts themself off from other children entirely by giving up social activities like sports or youth clubs and instead they begin to withdraw into themselves as they feel terrorised and alienated.

These are an example of some general problems that may occur as a child moves to a new school. There are many others such as bullying, but the problems that I have expanded are the main ones listed in the passage 'A gentle touch for the pupils sick of school.'

✓ Good focus on the key points, well expressed in your own writing.

The Reluctant Boarder.

Qu 2: The writer of the autobiography wants us to sympathize with the young boy. He seems to engage our sympathy through some of the vocabulary that is being used. Most of the vocabulary is very descriptive about the mother and the boy's feelings and in many cases actions.

The mother's feelings are shown when the mother says 'No, your name is Stephane and I want you to be called Stephane'. She says this when her son, the boy wants to change his name to Steve. I believe that the quote shows that the mother is feeling very insecure. She's upset, agitated and worried about leaving her son behind in the boarding school, but she felt that at least her son would still be Stephane and not Steve. I think that she may have felt that if he changed his name then he would change and he wouldn't be her little boy any more. Although changing his name may seem very insignificant, you can acknowledge that through this action you receive a very clear perspective of the mother's feelings and emotions, so we want to sympathise with her, for the possible loss that she may face, of her son.

The boy's feelings are shown in mainly two different ways. The first is when his mother is present and he decides to visit the lavatory, he then states 'I remember going to the lavatory and being confused by the wall of urinals - I had never seen any before.' This shows that the boy is feeling very confused in his new surroundings, upset that his mother has left him and insecure at the thought of being left in this new place, with no-one that he knew. He had never been away from his mother before. He also shows the boy playing with the tabby cat and hardly acknowledging the presence of his mother. I feel that this shows that the boy is putting on an act so as he doesn't upset his mother even more. I think that he is trying to believe that his mother wouldn't leave him, so I think he feels that this is all unreal and isn't really going to happen. He comes across as being calm and brave but you tend to feel sympathy towards the boy as he seems to be handling the situation well, but really we can see through his act, as readers, and understand his real feelings, i.e. fear, helplessness, loss and misunderstanding.

The second main way is the way in which he crumbles during the night when his mother leaves him. Through the use of the descriptive vocabulary you really can perceive what the boy is feeling. He states that he had shared a bed with his mother since he had been a baby. This is important as from this we can stem the trauma and anxiety that he is experiencing. He gets out of bed and looks for his mother. He calls out to her and when there is no answer he begins to cry. We feel real sympathy for the boy when he cries. This is because we try to empathise with the situation that he is in, and at such a young age i.e. 8. We acknowledge the fact that if put in his position we would probably have reacted in the same manner. We can perceive the fear and loss that he is feeling but most importantly, through the vocabulary we can see the shock and the sudden realisation, that he has lost his mother.

The vocabulary shows us details of events that occurred. These are important as they really do engage our sympathy. When the autobiography begins it states that the boy and his mother were the first to arrive. I think that we feel sympathy towards the boy then because he may be feeling slight embarrassment at being the first to arrive, especially as they arrived 3 hours early.

We also feel sympathy towards the boy when he unpacks his suitcase into a "tatty" wardrobe. It's the word tatty that seems to be the most significant as it gives and creates a picture in our heads of the wardrobe, and around this we can form a picture of the room. I feel that the room is very dark and dull. It's quite dusty and has very little furniture in it, apart from eleven rickety beds and six small tatty wardrobes. The majority of our own rooms are neatly furnished and contain our own possessions. We feel sympathy towards the boy because of the desolation in his dormitory, the bareness and the blankness. We can empathize with the boy because we wouldn't want to be in his position in our lives, yet in his it becomes our experience.

When he quotes "I remember needing to go to the lavatory and being confused by the wall of urinals - I had never seen any before." We can experience and see the shock and confusion that he is experiencing.

We also feel sorry for the boy when he makes friends with the school cat, Sausage. This event seems to insinuate that the boy wasn't able to make other friends, only the friendship of an animal, who can't return love in the same way as a human can.

We feel sorry for him when he goes in search for his mother and can't find her. All he finds instead is a dark, gloomy dormitory full of strangers and a man that he hardly knows who informs him that he won't be seeing his mother

for some time. That's when I feel that our sympathy reaches it's peak. This is because we are able to acknowledge the boy's loss and the way in which he has to become independant from his mother and begins to look after himself instead. We find this quite distressing that such a young boy should be removed from his mother when he is so dependant upon her.

These are the ways in which I feel that the writer of the autobiography has successfully written in a way which engages our sympathy through the use of events and vocabulary towards the boy.

The sentences and phrases also are of some significance. They are quite short and concise so as we can build up a picture in our minds of what is happening. But when the boy describes about himself the sentences are longer and tend to ramble. This makes us take pity on the boy as the more we read of his predicament, the more we sympathize with him.

These are the ways in which I feel that the sentences and phrases assist the writer of the autobiography to engage our sympathy towards the boy.

An excellent answer; a stylish focus on much of the detail and a real analysis of some of the language.
What you have to say about his mother is surely less relevant - the question asked about sympathy for the boy.

3,
Llanelli

16/9/36

Dear Mama,

How are you? I have settled in reasonably well. I miss you, but don't worry about me. I know I'm here because it's the best place for me.

I've made a friend! His name is Sausage. He's the school cat. He's fat and furry but he's a good friend to play with. He always likes to play.

I miss home so much. Everything is so confusing and new here. In the boys' lavatory there are urinals. They're white basin things that hang on the wall. We don't have them at home so I didn't really know what they were for. A boy teased me for not knowing, but a kind boy told me what they are for. It's a bit rude mama so I had better not tell you.

I'm the youngest boy by 2 years, so I'm finding it difficult to make any friends apart from Sausage. I'm not the only home-sick boy though. Sometimes when I lie in bed, looking into the darkness I can hear someone whimpering. I don't know who it is. All I know is that it's one of the 10 boys in my dormitory. I just wish I knew who, then we could be friends. No-one will tell me though as it isn't 'manly' to cry in the boys' opinions.

They still call me Stephane as you wanted. Brother Bede makes sure of that. I like Brother Bede, but not as much as I like you mama. The worst time that I missed you was on my first night here. I went in search of you from my bed as you weren't

there. I was confused because I couldn't find you. I ended up crying because you weren't anywhere. I then saw someone approaching. I thought it was you coming back for me, but it wasn't. It was Brother Bede. He had come to put me back to bed and he explained again what you had already told me.

I am coping with the work well. Brother Bede says that I am 'progressing sufficiently'. It seems sort of like home to me, but it will never be complete until you are here. I sometimes sit and wonder what you might be doing. I like to think of you sitting by the fire and rocking me to sleep whilst you sing a lullaby. That's what I dream about and it helps me to sleep on a night.

We do lots of exciting things here. I have a lot more opportunities now to do a lot more things than I ever used to. It can be good fun and I know that being here is what is best for me.

I think Sausage wants me to play with him now. He is making a lot of noise and is weaving around my ankles. Come and visit me soon mama, but don't worry about me as I'm well.

Yours

Stephane.

(and Sausage.)

(A)

Very good letter, totally empathising with the boy and developing accounts of the school life.

Examiner's commentary This candidate has clearly responded to the task with some excellent answers. However, the summary could be more concise and there is some irrelevance in the answer to the second question, especially where she has written about the mother's feelings. Always check that you are only doing what you need to do as this is what will be marked. In other respects, the answer is an excellent one from a candidate who certainly makes an effort to deal with the details of description and with the variety of types of statement about the events. The letter shows empathy with the character.

Good practice at speaking and listening will help you gain marks for your coursework (speaking and listening is always assessed during the course), and it will also help you make progress in other parts of your English.

Speaking and Listening are assessed in two kinds of ways. There are *general criteria* and there are *specific criteria* for the marks given. Let's have a look at what these terms mean:

General Criteria are statements about what you are expected to achieve in a number of different speaking and listening tasks. They are descriptions of your overall performance. Here is an example, the general criteria for grade B candidates:

Candidates speak purposefully in a range of contexts of increasing complexity, managing the contributions of others. They exhibit confidence and fluency in talk and show effective use of standard English vocabulary and grammar in a range of situations. They listen with some sensitivity and respond accordingly.

Specific Criteria are statements about three different uses of talk. These are:

i)   Explain, describe and narrate, for which the grade B criteria are:
   • *respond using a flexible range of vocabulary and grammatical structures to convey meaning, including inferential aspects;*
   • *manage challenging subject matter effectively.*

ii) Explore, analyse, imagine, for which the grade B criteria are:
   • *analyse and reflect effectively on real or imagined experience;*
   • *formulate and interpret information, developing significant points.*

iii) Discuss, argue, persuade, for which the grade B criteria are:
   • *manage collaborative tasks;*
   • *build on, and challenge the points made by others;*
   • *make probing contributions, structuring and organising points made by others.*

SPEAKING AND LISTENING TASKS

For **individual talks or presentations**, here is some advice: **plan** your main points in notes in order to **organise** your ideas, but not as a written essay – some talkers use index cards for their main points; the advantage of these is that you can keep them in order and discard them after each key point has been covered. Do not just talk, **communicate!** – use **eye contact**, change the **tone** and **pitch** of your voice, **pause** to give your listener a chance to take things in.

For **pair or group planning and discussion**: concentrate on the task; be prepared to express new possible ideas; be supportive of others – certainly you can be critical, but never become destructive; be prepared to change your mind and entertain the views of others; try to be sensitive to other students you are working with – take up their points and ideas, draw them out if necessary, agree with them, encourage them (and remember to do all this with appropriate "body language" such as eye contact and smiles); **never just express a point of view without reasons – always back it up with evidence**; and do not hog the conversation – let others have their say!

Listening

Sometimes it is easier to prepare yourself to speak and much more difficult to listen! In fact of all the things we do with language, listening may be the most difficult. How can you improve your listening skills?

The main approaches that you should practise are: **concentrate** as hard as you can on what is being said, and not so much on the way it is being said. As you are listening try not to be passive – this means that as well as taking in what you hear, you should actively be trying to think about what you hear. Other words for this skill are **analysing** or **interpreting**. Help the speaker through your own reactions and body language – remember that a good listener encourages a good speaker. Again, eye contact helps, as does an impression of concentration, perhaps nodding, smiling, agreeing. Above all do not become distracted and never put the speaker off by looking away or yawning!

Standard English

For all grades, you are required to use **Standard English**. What does this mean? Standard English is best described as English used for communication between groups of people. We may all use dialect, a kind of local language, but it is generally accepted that in the world of business, education, communication and work, there is a generally accepted form of speech which can be recognised by most people as a common form of the language. In a sense, **Standard English is the language of public communication**.

You are not assessed on your accent, and do not try to use long words just for the sake of impressing others. But you are expected to speak in a register of standard English suitable for some situations in life. These might be formal or informal occasions, although you will obviously speak more informally amongst friends on less serious matters.

The most important thing to remember is that you must **communicate** and **express** your points well. It goes without saying that pupils who are interested in the world around them have more ideas to communicate!

Getting the ideas in the first place

As you go through your GCSE course, try to develop your views on important **issues in the news, or on controversial and moral topics**. You cannot possibly hope to do well in any speaking and listening tasks unless you have **ideas** of your own. Here are a few issues at random – what would your views be?: should the police be armed?; are test tube babies morally acceptable?; should whaling be banned?; is there a case for a federal Europe?

Knowledge about spoken language

In your exam you may be asked to comment on the way that spoken language works: this is a part of the National Curriculum in English known as **knowledge about language**. It is more likely that you would be asked to comment on examples of speech from a play or extracts of dialogue from scripts.

These are the kinds of things you should be thinking about: how language changes over time; how words and parts of words are borrowed from other languages; how new words come into existence and come to be popular in current usage; influences on spoken (and written) language; attitudes to language use; the differences between speech and writing; differences between the vocabulary and grammar of Standard English and dialects.

Here are some useful terms to remember, all of which are referred to in the glossary on pages 9–13:

Standard English	Intonation	Slang
Dialect	Mockery	Jargon
Accent	Dialogue	Tone
Register	Monologue	

This last section of the book is designed to give you as many chances as possible to practise your skills. For English, practice may not always make perfect but it does give you a chance to think and improve and is probably the best way there is to revise.

This section is split into two parts. The first part has a selection of tasks, many of which are taken from GCSE exam papers, and the second part contains Examiner's tips which advise you on how to approach the various tasks.

Each task has a brief introduction, followed by some stimulus material and then the task itself. Please have a go at the tasks first and then read the tips to see if your approach is what was expected. If you are way out of line with what was expected you might then choose to have another go. Practise hard and good luck with your examination!

TASK 1

We have looked at literary stimulus already: here is a chance to practise yourself. Read the poem "Head of English" which is printed on the accompanying sheet of paper. When you have read it carefully answer the questions which follow it.

STIMULUS MATERIAL

Head of English
by Carol Ann Duffy

Today we have a poet in the class
A real live poet with a published book.
Notice the inkstained fingers girls. Perhaps
we're going to witness verse hot from the press.
5 Who knows. Please show your appreciation
by clapping. Not too loud. Now

sit up straight and listen. Remember
the lesson on assonance, for not all poems
sadly, rhyme these days. Still. Never mind.
10 Whispering's, as always, out of bounds –
but do feel free to raise some questions.
After all, we're paying forty pounds.

Those of you with English Second Language
see me after break. We're fortunate
15 to have this person in our midst.
Season of mists and so on and so forth.
I've written quite a bit of poetry myself,
am doing Kipling with the Lower Fourth.

Right. That's enough from me. On with the Muse.
20 Open a window at the back. We don't
want winds of change about the place.
Take notes, but don't write reams. Just an essay
on the poet's themes. Fine. Off we go.
Convince us that there's something we don't know.

25 Well. Really. Run along now girls. I'm sure
that gave us an insight to an outside view.
Applause will do. Thank you
very much for coming here today. Lunch
in the hall? Do hang about. Unfortunately
30 I have to dash. Tracey will show you out.

1   a. What seems to you to be the attitude of the teacher to the poet who is visiting the class?

    b. Look at the various instructions which are given to the pupils in the class and explain how, as a member of the class, you would react to them. Give reasons for your points.

    c. Certain words and phrases in the poem tell us things about the type of poetry which the teacher prefers. Pick out those words and phrases and suggest what they tell you.

2   Imagine that you are the poet. You get home and are talking to someone about your day. Describe your experience in the lesson.

NEAB 1995

All English syllabuses contain a requirement for reading and working on writing from other cultures. What that means is that you are expected to read stories, poems and so on from cultures other than those which are defined as the English Literary Heritage in the National Curriculum.

The story which follows, which is taken from a book of American short stories, is called "Motel Chronicles (an excerpt)" and is by Sam Shepard. The collection of pieces from which this little story is taken is, in part, observations, poems and thoughts that are a background to a film of his.

Read the story carefully.

Motel Chronicles (an excerpt)
by Sam Shepard

The first time I ran away from school I was ten. Two older guys talked me into it. They were brothers and they'd both been in and out of Juvenile Hall five times. They told me it would just be like taking a short vacation. So I went. We stole three bikes out of a back yard and took off for the Arroyo Seco. The bike I stole was too big for me so I could never sit up on the seat all the way. I pedalled standing.

We hid the bikes in a stand of Eucalyptus trees at the edge of the Arroyo and went down to the creek. We caught Crawdads with marshmallow bait then tore the shells off them and used their meat to catch more Crawdads. When lunch time came I had to share my lunch with the brothers because they'd forgotten to bring theirs. I spread the contents of the paper bag out on a big flat rock. A carrot wrapped in wax paper with a rubber band around it. A meatloaf sandwich. A melted bag of M and Ms. They ate the M and Ms first. Tore the package open and licked the chocolate off the paper. They offered me a lick but I declined. I didn't eat any of the meatloaf sandwich either. I always hated meatloaf. Especially cold and between bread.

The rest of the afternoon we climbed around in the hills looking for snakes until one of them got the idea of lowering our bikes down into the aqueduct and riding along the dry bed until we reached Los Angeles. I said 'yes' to everything even though I suspected LA was at least a hundred miles away. The only other time I'd ever been to Los Angeles was when my Aunt took me to the Farmer's Market in her '45 Dodge to look at the Myna birds. I must have been six then.

I climbed the chain-link barrier fence while the two brothers took the tension out of the barb-wire strands at the top. Enough so I could straddle the fence, get one foot on the concrete wall of the aqueduct and drop some ten or twelve feet to the bottom. Then they lowered the bikes down to me, suspended on their belts. We rode for miles down this giant corridor of cement, the wheels of our bikes bumping over the brown lines of caulking used to seal the seams. Except for those seams it was the smoothest, flattest surface I'd ever ridden a bike on.

We rode past red shotgun shells faded by the sun, dead opossums, beer cans, Walnut shells, Carob pods, a Raccoon with two babies, pages out of porno magazines, hunks of rope, inner tubes, hub caps, bottle caps, dried-up Sage plants, boards with nails, stumps, roots, smashed glass, yellow golf balls with red stripes, a lug wrench, women's underwear, tennis shoes, dried-up socks, a dead dog, mice, Dragon Flies screwing in mid-air, shrivelled-up frogs with their eyes popped out. We rode for miles until we came to a part that was all enclosed like a big long tunnel and we couldn't see light at the other end. We stopped our bikes and stared through the mouth of that tunnel and I could tell they were just as scared as I was even though they were older. It was already starting to get dark and the prospect of getting stuck in there at night, not knowing how long the thing was or what town we'd come out in or how in the hell we were going to climb back out once we came to the end of it, had us all wishing we were back home. None of us said we wished that but I could feel it passing between us.

I don't remember how the decision was made but we pushed off straight ahead into it. The floor was concave and slick with moss, causing the wheels to slip sideways. Sometimes our feet came down ankle-deep in sludge and black mud and we ended up having to walk the bikes through most of it. We kept making sounds to each other just to keep track of where we were as the light disappeared behind us. We started out trying to scare each other with weird noises but gave it up because the echoes were truly terrifying. I kept having visions of Los Angeles appearing suddenly at the other end of the tunnel. It would just pop up at us, all blinking with lights and movement and life. Sometimes it would appear like I'd seen it in postcards. (Palm Trees set against a background of snowy mountains with orange groves sprawling beneath them. The Train Station with a burro standing in front of it, harnessed to a cart.) But it didn't come. For hours it didn't come. And my feet were wet. And I forgot what the two brothers even looked like anymore. I kept having terrible thoughts about home. About what would happen when I finally got back. In the blackness I pictured our house. The red awning. The garage door. The strip of lawn down the centre of the driveway. The Pyracantha berries. The Robins that ate them. Close-ups of the Robin's beak guzzling red berries. So close I could see little dribbles of dirt from wet lawns where he'd been pulling out worms. I couldn't stop these pictures. (Me walking to school. The chubby old Crossing Guard at the corner with his round wooden sign that read STOP in red letters. The dirt playground. Porcelain water fountains with silver knobs dribbling. The face of the kid I hit in the stomach for no reason. Little traces of mayonnaise around his lips.) I had the feeling these pictures would drown me. I wondered what the two brothers were thinking but I never asked them.

It was night when we reached the end and it wasn't Los Angeles either. Huge Sycamore trees with hazy orange street lights loomed over our heads. We could hear the sound of a freeway. Periodic whooshing of trucks. We hauled ourselves out by climbing on each other's shoulders and hooking the belts to the top of the fence. The oldest brother said he recognized the town we were in. He said it was Sierra Madre and he had an Uncle who lived pretty close by. We pedalled to his Uncle's house and we weren't talking to each other at that point. There was nothing to say.

His Uncle lived in a small three-room house with several men sitting around the front room drinking beer and watching the Lone Ranger on TV. Nobody seemed surprised to see us. They acted like this had happened a lot before. A woman was making a big pot of spaghetti in the kitchen and she gave us each a paper plate and told us to wait for the meat sauce to heat up. We sat on the floor at the feet of the men in the front room and watched the Lone Ranger and ate spaghetti. That was the first time I'd ever seen TV because we didn't have one at home. (My Dad said we didn't need one.) I liked the Lone Ranger a lot. Especially the music when he galloped on Silver and reared up waving his hat at a woman holding a baby.

We were finally caught later that night by a squad car on a bridge in South Pasadena. The cops acted like we were adults. They had that kind of serious tone: 'Where did you get these bikes? What are your names? Where do you live? Do you know what time it is?' Stuff like that. They radioed our parents and confiscated the bikes. My mother showed up and drove me back, explaining how my Dad was so pissed off that he wouldn't come because he was afraid he'd kill me. She kept saying, 'Now you've got a Police Record. You'll have that the rest of your life.'

I got whipped three times with the buckle-end of my Dad's belt. Three times. That was it. Then he left the house. He never said a word.

I lay in bed listening to my mother ironing in the kitchen. I pictured her ironing. The hiss of steam. The sprinkle bottle she used to wet my Dad's shirts. I pictured her face staring down at the shirt as her arm moved back and forth in a steady tempo.

TASK

1 The story is written in a style which causes us to be very involved in the story. Choose three moments which you consider to be important. Briefly describe them and explain your reactions to them.

2 The place names in this story are clearly American but there are a whole host of details which put this story clearly in its American setting and culture. Explain what, for you, gives the story its American feel.

TASK 3

You are sometimes given quite a lot of stimulus material and the first thing to do is to read it carefully. When examiners set a paper they consider the length of the stimulus material and make allowances for the time you will take to read it. So do not worry if you spend some time reading and thinking – you must do this before you start writing.

This question paper is based on newspaper articles about the problems which can be caused by difficult neighbours. Before you read them, look at the tasks you have to do at the end of the stimulus material. Think about these tasks as you read the articles. You may, if you wish, make notes alongside them and underline or highlight anything that helps you plan your answers.

Spitting Distance
BRITAIN'S WORST NEIGHBOURS

STIMULUS MATERIAL

If an Englishman's home is his castle, what happens when Mr and Mrs Genghis Khan move in next door? What about Miss Saturday Night Party, Mr Midnight Strimmer or Mrs That's My Parking Space? Or even Mr and Mrs Slightly Irritating But They Will Do It Again And Again?

Nobody would ever admit to being the neighbours from hell, but a lot of people think they're living next door to them (and often the feeling is mutual).

"The only way to describe it is torture," said Jean Hughes. So irritating was her experience with a Miss South-East London Ghetto Blaster that she set up the Right to Peace and Quiet Campaign. "Often when you complain, they realise they have got some power over you, the power to do it again. And then you end up living your life in constant fear of something happening."

The kind of fear that is the constant companion of the Thompson family, who live on a council estate. Sidney and his wife, Thelma, are both in their seventies and have lived in the same end-of-terrace house for 25 years. It was always an ordinary kind of place – respectable working-class, if you will – and full of the kind of noise and boisterousness you'd expect. But it was pleasant.

Until, that is, last November, when the Pope family moved in next door. That they had eight children was nothing out of the ordinary – the Thompsons had had nine. That they had Rottweilers... well, again, they're scarcely uncommon around there. But four of them?

The Popes quickly made their mark. Nothing spectacular, mind, just persistent noise, barrages of verbal abuse, daily fights among themselves, and a garden so full of dog excrement that the Thompsons called in an environmental health officer. The kind of things that, taken in isolation, are no more than a nuisance – if they happen occasionally. But they happened round the clock, and, said Mr Thompson, "If you ask the Popes to be quiet, they just jeer and clap their hands." The family on the other side of the Popes, who had lived there for 16 years, moved away. Another neighbour, who refused to be identified, even went so far as to purchase an air pistol to protect herself, although a second liked the Popes so much that she has moved in with them.

Now the Popes, too, are finding themselves sinned against: their windows were mysteriously smashed one night earlier this month. Around the same time, encouraged by Pope children, the Pope dogs chased three children from open land. Baseball bats were waved. The police were called in the middle of the night.

Why had the Popes been moved there in the first place? "They were homeless and we had an obligation to rehouse them," said a council official earlier this year. And why were they homeless? Because their previous council house had burnt down. It took four fire teams to tackle the blaze. "I've never seen a house so damaged so quickly," said the fire chief at the time. And why did the Popes have to remain next door to the Thompsons? Because it was a condition of Mr and Mrs Pope's bail. And what were they out on bail for? Arson.

Not that such conflicts are the preserve of council estates. Them Next Door versus Us In Here is probably the reason laws were first laid down.

"Your next-door neighbour," wrote G K Chesterton more than 70 years ago, "is not a man; he is an environment. He is the barking of a dog; he is the noise of a pianola; he is a dispute about a party wall; he is drains that are worse than yours, or roses that are better than yours."

Listen to John McVicar, the journalist and, let's face it, former bank robber. Even he is not immune to the temptations of the neighbourhood watch-it. "A girl upstairs flooded my place with her washing machine and we had a big row about it."

Later, he had a run-in with another neighbour. "She tried to nick my parking place. So I blocked her off. She nipped out of her car, ran over and let my tyres down. So I let hers down."

If Jean Hughes was ever tempted to retaliate, she kept her counsel, but the road to her founding the Right to Peace and Quiet Campaign was a long and noisy one. Particularly, she will never forget her neighbour's favourite record, Lisa Stansfield's All Around The World. "I could hear it right through the wall just about every day – word for word for word. And it's not as if I didn't like Lisa Stansfield's music. I love listening to her, but when I choose to listen to her." As Hughes pointed out, loud music is a potent form of torture. When the Americans wanted to winkle out General Noriega, they bombarded him with festival-strength heavy rock.

Hughes found herself wondering about the psychology of such neighbours from hell. "People should look at it," she says. "Often it's to do with status. They feel they don't have it, and it's a way of getting back at the people next door. My neighbour was a single mother and probably felt jealous as I was buying my council house. Also, playing music at that level gives you a bit of a buzz, like going to a disco." Both she and her partner – her word – are DJs. "That buzz can be important for people who can't get out much. And it can be addictive."

The psychology of the next-door neighbour is something that has often crossed the mind of New Zealand-born dentist, David Benson. Some 17 years ago, he moved into a Wiltshire village. He has one big bugbear in his life, 10 years of disruption and confusion, occasioned, in the view of Benson and other people in the village, by his neighbour, the wife of the local vicar. As so often, when put down on paper, the details of the complaints look trivial, even silly. Apple bombardments, late-night lawn mowing and hedge trimming, a running row about the use of the lane for parking. Eventually, of course, it became something of a two-way thing. In some ways, the details are almost irrelevant. The point is that they went on and on, starting in 1984, and that other villagers also suffered abuse.

His wife, Sue, is more philosophical about it all, or maybe just more resigned. "It bothers

David more than me. It's intruding on his male territory. But if only the Church had come to us a couple of years ago and said, 'Please be patient'."

At this point it is worth mentioning that the teaching 'Love Your Neighbour' appears in many religions. We've all heard it. It's the doing of it that's just about impossible.

(Adapted from an article by Peter Silverton in *The Observer* ©)

Hate Thy Neighbour

May 1993. Emma Greensmith, a grandmother, was found guilty of playing Jim Reeves records 18 hours a day. Her hi-fi was seized and visitors were barred from her house between the hours of 9pm and 9am.

November 1992. Nigel and Sonia Hicks were evicted after 14 months of an onslaught against their neighbours. They hopped along in front of a crippled war veteran, Jack Tilting, yelling abuse. They stuck a rude poster in their window, chopped wood and played loud music in the early hours. They were sent to separate hostels.

January 1990. John Eales became so fed up with his neighbour that he drilled holes in his floor and poured petrol through them to the flat below. He was given a conditional discharge.

June 1992. Donald Jeffers was arrested for his own safety and bound over for 18 months for his terrorising of his neighbour, Veronica Edwards. He'd complained her budgies were noisy and reported her to the RSPCA. He'd told her teenage son she was a witch, dumped grass cuttings over her fence and photographed her at the washing line.

April 1990. After blitzing neighbours for two years with junk mail, Tracey Davies was given a conditional discharge, and ordered to pay £10 costs and £50 compensation.

November 1991. Bert and Mary Stanley, both 75, banged on their ceiling if anyone walked on the floor above, hurled abuse at neighbours strolling in the street, called the police to a noisy party at which everyone was, in fact, asleep, and terrified a couple into watching TV with the sound off. The council offered 17 witnesses.

September 1991. In a dispute over a parking space, Joanne and Fred Cooper were alleged to have menaced the family of 'That's Life's' Howard Leader with lumps of wood, and threatened to shoot a neighbour's cat and nail it to the door if it came near their aviary.

STIMULUS
MATERIAL

Battle lines: John Gladden's home improvements have left him at odds with his Norbury neighbours and his local council.

TASK

1   You have been asked to write the words for an information leaflet on behalf of the *Right to Peace and Quiet Campaign*. By referring to the article "Spitting Distance", the photograph and the material headed "Hate Thy Neighbour":

(a)   summarise the things people do which annoy and upset their neighbours.

(b)   explain the reasons given in the material for neighbours behaving so badly.   (20)

Write in paragraphs using your own words.
You should write about 200–250 words altogether.

2   How does the writer try to make "Spitting Distance" interesting and entertaining?
In your answer you should consider:

●   the incidents and the characters he describes

●   his choice of words in the article.   (20)

MEG 1995

This example is taken from a Personal and Imaginative Writing Section of an NEAB (Northern) paper set in 1995.

● Answer one question in this section.

● You should spend about one hour on this section and write about 3 sides.

● The material provided may give you ideas to use in planning and writing, but you should develop your writing in the way you think is best.

Either

1   (a) Write a story where a dare plays an important part.

Or

      (b) Write about an occasion when you carried out a dare.

Or

2   Write a story in which a child encounters a startling or unusual adult character.

      This extract is taken from *Great Expectations* by Charles Dickens and describes Miss Havisham.

> She was dressed in rich materials – satins, and lace, and silks – all of white. Her shoes were white. And she had a long white veil dependent from her hair, and she had bridal flowers in her hair, but her hair was white. Some jewels sparkled on her neck and on her hands, and some other jewels lay sparkling on the table. Dresses, less splendid than the dress she wore, and half packed trunks, were scattered about. She had not quite finished dressing, for she had but one shoe on – the other was on the table near her hand – her veil was but half arranged, her watch and chain were not put on, and some lace for her bosom lay with those trinkets, and with her handkerchief, and gloves, and some flowers, and a prayerbook, all confusedly heaped about the looking glass.

NEAB 1995

TASK 5

Earlier in this book we used an example of a fairly short answer comprehension test and this is what we have here. What is printed below is one section of the examination paper. We have reproduced it almost exactly as it appeared because the questions take you systematically through the story referring to particular lines.

Read carefully the short story below. Then answer **all** the questions which follow.

Some Day My Prince Will Come

STIMULUS MATERIAL

It's Saturday. Working on the House Day. Every weekend Martin works on the house. Weekends of fogs of dust and muffled curses from the closed door behind which he toils… of tripping over the plumbing pipes and searching for one small sandal in the rubble and keeping out of Daddy's way.

5 Anyway, that Saturday I got up and fed the children and peeled the plasticine from Martin's hammer before he saw it. Really, compared to the rest of the week, weekends were such a strain. I pulled a nail out of Tilly's shoe and she made such a fuss that I tried to shut her up by telling her a story. And Adam fell down and shrieked so badly that Martin heard him over the electric sander.

After lunch Martin went out. He had all these errands to do on Saturdays, like getting his hair 10 cut and things mended that I had forgotten to do during the week or that I had been far too busy to fetch. He can't understand that I'm busy, when there's nothing to show for it. No floors relaid, nothing like that. And he has to go to all these proper little shops with old men in overalls who take hours; he refuses to go to the big help-yourself places because he says they're soulless.

It was two thirty and raining outside. The afternoon stretched ahead; Adam was staggering 15 around, scattering wood shavings. Then I looked in the paper and saw that "Snow White" was on. So I wrote a note to Martin and heaved out the double buggy.

"Does Snow White wear a beautiful pink dress?" Tilly asked. She's obsessed with pink.

"Can't remember," I said. "I was your age when I saw it. I loved it more than any other film I've ever seen."

20 "Snow White gets deaded," said Adam.

"She doesn't!" I cried. "She's only asleep. She wakes when the Prince comes along and kisses her."

When did Martin last kiss me? Properly. Or when, indeed, did I last kiss him?

We arrived at the cinema. A peeling brick cliff, its neon lights glaring over the grey street. How 25 could such buildings house such impossible dreams?

Inside I saw *him* for the first time in ten years. I saw him straight away. I had sat next to him in fifty cinema seats. Him beside me, his arm lying along the back of the seat. But now his arms were flung each side of his children.

The cinema darkened. Snow White was washing the steps, scrubbing and singing. I thought: 30 forgot the Daz and now I've missed the shops.

"When's the Prince coming?" hissed Tilly. "Will he come on his horse?"

"Of course."

He'd had a motorbike. I'd sat behind him, gripping him with my arms, my face pressed against the leather. My parents were terrified that I would marry him. But I didn't, did I? All I'd heard 35 was that he was married and had two children. She was called Joyce. With a name like that she must be overweight.

The Dark Queen was up on the screen with her bitter, beautiful face. A hand gripped mine.

"She's horrid," said Tilly.

"She's jealous," I whispered.

40 The hand squeezed. "She's turning into a witch."

"I don't like her," I said.

Tilly said in her posh voice, "It's because she's got ugly thoughts." I had a sudden desire to grip my growing wayward girl and protect her from what lay ahead. But she disliked shows of emotion.

45   Snow White let in the witch. As she took the apple, the audience sat absolutely still. All those children – not a sweet paper rustled. Nothing.

    When she bit the apple, Tilly hid her face.

    "It's all right," I said desperately. "I told you, the Prince will come."

    He came of course, as you knew he would. The Prince knelt down to kiss Snow White. And
50 then she was in his arms and he was lifting her onto his horse. Not a motorbike – a stallion of pure white, and the sun cast long shadows between the trees as they rode off, and ahead lay the castle, radiant.

    "Where's your hanky?' I muttered.

    I took her handkerchief and blew my nose. The lights came on.

55   "Don't be soppy," said Tilly. "It's only a story."

    Twenty minutes later I was walking up our street. The eye of the bedroom window looked at me and said: Shouldn't have gone, should you?

    The car was outside and the lights were on. Martin must be home. The rain stopped but I wiped my face on my sleeve. He would just think my face was wet from the rain. If, that is, he
60 noticed anything about me.

    I went into the house. There was a forest of planks in the hall. He had been to the timber merchant. Martin didn't come out of the kitchen. No buzzing drill. I hesitated. Could he read my thoughts?

    Then I thought: He's made me a surprise.

65   I stood still and let the realization fill me, through my limbs, like warm liquid.

    Martin had made the supper. Hopelessly, because he can't cook. But he had cleared the table and bought a bottle of wine and lots of expensive things from the delicatessen. He realized how I'd been feeling lately.

    I opened the door. But this wasn't a story. Life is not that neat, is it? No fairy tale.

70   There sat Martin, with a can of beer in front of him and the lunch plates still piled in the sink. Packets were heaped on the table; not exotic cheeses but boxes of screws and nails.

    He looked up. "Didn't hear you come in."

    "Exhausted?" I asked.

    He nodded. Fiction is shapely. A story billows out like a sheet, then comes the final knot. The
75 End. Against the pink sky stands a castle, lit from within. The End.

    A silence as he poured the beer into his glass. He said, "The end is in sight. I think I can finally say I've finished this bloody kitchen."

(Adapted from "Some Day My Prince Will Come" by Deborah Moggach)

Look again at lines 1–16

TASK

1 What are your first impressions of the writer and the life she leads? Give reasons for your opinions.   (10)

Look again at lines 17–55

2 The writer comes out of the cinema in tears. What happens to make her so upset? Why do you think she reacts as she does?   (10)

Look again at lines 56–77

3 What happens after the writer leaves the cinema? What do you think about this as an ending to the story?   (10)

To answer the next question you will need to think about the story as a whole.

4 What do you think about the relationship between the writer and her husband, Martin? Give reasons for your opinions.   (10)

WJEC 1994

TASK 6

This 1995 paper gave a chance to do a variety of writing. First of all there is a picture and then there are three associated possible tasks. In this case each of the tasks requires a different style of writing. The first is a particularly personal piece of writing; the second gives you a chance to develop a story which needs an effective central character; the third is a piece of discursive writing where you are asked to develop an argument. You might like to practise by doing all three tasks and then deciding which task you felt you coped with best and was most satisfying.

STIMULUS MATERIAL

TASK

FIRST **Look at the picture above.**
It shows people in hospital during visiting time.
NEXT Think about times you have been in hospitals as a patient, or a visitor.

WHAT YOU HAVE TO WRITE

1 **Describe** as vividly as you can

   either (a) an experience you have had as a hospital patient,
   or (b) an occasion when you visited someone in hospital.

   OR

2 **Write a short story** in which the main character is someone working in a hospital.

   OR

3 "Good health is the responsibility of the individual."
   Write your views on this statement.

SEB 1995

The next example that we are taking from a 1994 examination paper involves quite a substantial amount of reading and we suggest that you tackle one question which needs careful reading and analysis to complete it successfully.

When the writer was a boy, he lived in the countryside with his father on the island of Trinidad in the West Indies. After his father's death, he moved with his mother to Port-of-Spain, the island's capital city.

I had always considered this woman, my mother, as the enemy. She was sure to misunderstand anything I did, and the time came when I thought she not only misunderstood me, but quite definitely disapproved of me. I was an only child, but for her I was one too many.

She hated my father, and even after he died she continued to hate him.

She would say, 'Go ahead and do what you are doing. You are your father's child, you hear, not mine.'

My mother had decided to leave my father, and she wanted to take me to her mother. I refused to go.

My father was ill, and in bed. Besides, he had promised that if I stayed with him I was to have a whole box of crayons.

I chose the crayons and my father.

In fact, my mother moved us to Port-of-Spain where I saw what the normal relationship was between the beater and the beaten – when I saw this I was grateful.

My mother made a great thing at first about keeping me in my place and knocking out all the nonsense my father had taught me. I don't know why she didn't try harder, but the fact is that she soon lost interest in me, and she let me run about the street, only rushing down to beat me from time to time.

Occasionally, though, she would take the old firm line.

One day, she kept me home. She said, 'No school for you today. I am sick of tying your shoelaces for you. Today you will have to learn that!'

I didn't think she was being fair. After all, in the country none of us wore shoes and I wasn't used to them.

That day she beat me and beat me and made me tie knot after knot and in the end I still couldn't tie my shoelaces.

Still there were surprising glimpses of kindness.

There was the time, for instance, when I was cleaning some tumblers for her one Saturday morning. I dropped a tumbler and it broke. Before I could do anything about it my mother saw what had happened.

She said, 'How did you break it?'

I said, 'It just slipped off. It was smooth smooth.'

She said, 'A lot of nonsense drinking from glass. They break so easy.'

And that was all. I got worried about my mother's health.

She was never worried about mine.

She thought that there was no illness in the world a stiff dose of hot Epsom Salts couldn't cure.

And if there was something she couldn't understand, she sent me to the Health Office in Tragerete Road. That was an awful place. You waited and waited before you went in to see the doctor.

My mother considered the Health Office a good place for me to go to. I would go there at eight in the morning and return any time after two in the afternoon. It kept me out of mischief, and it only cost twenty-four cents a year.

But you mustn't get the impression that I was a saint all the time. I wasn't. I used to have odd fits where I just couldn't take an order from anybody, particularly my mother. I used to feel that I would dishonour myself for life if I took anybody's orders. And life is a funny thing, really. I sometimes got these fits just when my mother was anxious to be nice to me.

I wrote an essay for my schoolmaster on the subject, 'A Day at the Seaside'. I don't think any schoolmaster ever got an essay like that. I talked about how I was nearly drowned and how calmly I was facing death, with my mind absolutely calm, thinking, 'Well, boy, this is the end.' The teacher was so pleased he gave me ten marks out of twelve.

He said, 'You are a genius.'

When I went home and told my mother, 'That essay I wrote today, I got ten out of twelve for it.'

My mother said, 'How do you lie so in front of my face? You want me to give you a slap to turn your face?'

In the end I convinced her.

She melted at once. She sat down in the hammock and said, 'Come and sit down by me, son.'

Just then the crazy fit came on me.

I got very angry for no reason at all and I said, 'No, I – not going to sit by you.'

She laughed and coaxed.

And the angrier she made me.

Slowly the friendliness died away. It had become a struggle between two wills. I was prepared to drown rather than dishonour myself by obeying.

'I told you to come and sit here.'

'I am not sitting down.'

'Take off your belt.'

I took it off and gave it to her. She belted me soundly, and my nose bled, but still I didn't sit in the hammock.

At times like this I used to cry, without meaning it, 'If my father was here you wouldn't be behaving like this.'

So she remained the enemy. She was someone from whom I was going to escape as soon as I grew big enough. That was, in fact, the main lure of adulthood.

I was travelling by bus, one of the green buses of Sam's Super Service, from Port-of-Spain to Petit Valley.

My head felt as though it would split, but when I tried to shout out I found I couldn't open my mouth. I tried again, but all I heard, more distinctly now, was the constant chattering.

Water was pouring down my face.

I was flat out under a tap and there were faces above me looking down.

Someone said, 'How you feeling?'

I said, trying to laugh, 'I feel all right.'

A voice asked, 'You have any pains?'

I shook my head.

But suddenly, my whole body began to ache. I tried to move my hand and it hurt.

I said, 'I think I've broken my hand.'

But I could stand, and they made me walk into the house.

My mother came and I could see her glassy and wet with tears.

Somebody, I cannot remember who, said, 'Boy, you had your mother really worried.'

I looked at her tears, and I felt I was going to cry too. I had discovered that she could be worried and anxious for me.

TASK Write down separately the advice you would give the mother, and the advice you would give to the boy, to help them to improve their relationship.

ULEAC 1994

Advice for the boy

I realise that it is a hard time for you, losing your father and then moving from the countryside to the city with a woman called your mother, which you hardly even know.

You have got to remember that your mother is trying her best to look after you and it is hard for her too. She may not show it but she does care for you and you don't make it easy for her.

When she asks you to do something, don't be disobedient and start arguing with her. Just do it no matter how strange. This way you both have an easy life.

I know it was wrong of her to question you about your school grades but this was only because she cares about you and does not want you lying to her.

You say yourself that your mother is sometimes anxious to be nice to you but you go into fits. It would be easier if you didn't go into these fits on purpose and accept it when she is nice to you however hard this may be.

You say that she does not care about you but she must do you she sends you to the Health Office. When you were ill on the bus and you returned home your mother was crying this proves that she cares for you.

Please don't argue with her it is obvious that you both care for eachother. So don't argue, talk to each other and hopefully one day you and your mother will be as close as you were with your father.

Task 7

Advice for the mother.

The first thing which you have got to remember is that countryside life is different to city life, so you need to give him time to adjust to this new way of life.

Remember that his father has just died so it is a very distressing time for the boy. It will be hard for him to come and live with someone he does not know very well and accept it.

The boy feels that you don't love him and you have lost interest in him. You must show that you have it. Take an interest in the things he does, believe him when he tells you he has done well at school, show affection to him without questioning him first.

I know it may be hard for you to love him when he talks about his father all the time, and you obviously did not feel the same way about his father. However you cannot go around saying bad things about him in front of the boy, because the boy will not like this, due to the fact he still loves him and it will probably make him hate you even more.

The last thing you have got to remember is not to beat him when he has done something wrong but talk to him and explain what he has done is wrong.

It may take time but if you follow the advice given to you, you will soon become like a proper family.

You are sometimes given quite a lot of stimulus material and the first thing to do is to read it carefully. When the examiners set a paper they consider the length of the stimulus material and make allowances for the time that you will take to read it. So do not worry if you spend some time reading and thinking – you must do this before you start writing.

This stimulus material and the questions which follow are based on the idea of "WORKING AWAY". In the past few years cheaper air travel and fewer passport controls or restrictions on where people can go have encouraged many young people to travel abroad. More recently, the abolition of many employment requirements within the European Community has made it possible to find work in other countries as well.

Printed below you will find a leaflet about working abroad. You will also find details of four possible jobs. Read this material carefully and make use of it to answer the questions which follow.

WANTING TO WORK AWAY THIS SUMMER?

FOLLOW THESE DOs AND DON'Ts FOR SUCCESS AND SAFETY

Every year thousands of young people find jobs in other parts of Europe and now, with the opening of Eastern European countries to foreigners, there are more opportunities than ever to live in other communities and to see different places.

DO ✓

Find a job before you set off.

Make sure your terms of employment are clearly set out in writing.

Look around and find work which suits your personality and abilities.

Buy a return ticket so that if things go wrong you can leave.

Apply for work through student organisations or well-known agencies.

Check whether you need a permit or visa of any kind before you set off.

Apply for several jobs and compare what they can offer you.

DON'T ✗

Take the first job you see.

Break your agreements. It makes it more difficult for others next time.

Expect jobs to be easy. You're cheap, casual labour and will be made to work hard.

Leave arrangements to the last minute.

Take work offers from people at airports and railway stations.

Ignore local employment laws and regulations.

To find out more about job opportunities in Europe and America look in student magazines or contact your nearest agency.

A

PARENTS PLUS – FRANCE
10 Orwell Road, Felixstowe,
Suffolk IP7 2RQ
(Tel: 0394 46201)

AU PAIRS, and **NANNIES** can be placed by this organisation with families all over France. Monthly salaries of up to £350. Board and accommodation is provided by the family. Minimum age 18 years. Minimum length of stay usually 6–12 months, but during the summer, from June until September, there are vacancies for 3 months and a few for 1–2 months' stays, applications for which should be made between April and June. Write to the Organiser at the above address giving full details of availability.

B

HOTEL "STROMBOLI": Corso Mameli No. 78, 30850 Verbania Intra (Novara), Italy

WAITING STAFF. £63 per month. To work from 09.30–15.00 and 18.30–21.00 (including meal breaks) 6 days per week. Free board and accommodation provided. Period of work from July 1st–September 30th: minimum period of work 1 month, which must not end between August 1st and 20th.

Applications to Signora Carmine Gianna at the above address

C

MARQUEE HOLIDAYS LIMITED

**Courier Department
189 Bath Road
Basingstoke
Hants
☎ 0256 92220**

RESIDENTIAL COURIERS (pre university students and undergraduates) to work on camp sites. Wages around £100 per week. Duties are varied but in short they involve welcoming and looking after customers, helping with any problems that may arise and maintaining tents and equipment. Accommodation and cooking facilities provided in large frame tents. Candidates are required to be proficient in French or Italian: experience in working with people and camping is desirable. Must be fit, responsible and self-reliant. Periods of work either from the end of April to mid-July or early July to the end of September.

☛ *Write to Mr G Small at the above address*

D

CENTRO AMUNO DI STUDI PREISTORICI: 25044 Capo di Ponte, Brescia, Italy

VOLUNTEERS (*5 positions*) to work for an archaeological institute specialising in the study of prehistoric rock art. The work involves editing, translating and working in the laboratory and library. Applicants should have an interest in archaeology, anthropology and/or art history, and have a good command of at least two languages – English, Italian, French, Spanish or German. Free accommodation and one meal per day provided. 5 days per week for a minimum of 2 months; dates of work by arrangement.

Applications to Erica Simoes de Abreu at the above address.

1   Read the notes below which describe the qualifications and interests of five young people. Giving your reasons, state which of the **four jobs described on the insert** each of them **could** apply for. Briefly say which job you think they would be most suited for. **The first one is done for you to show how to set out your answer.**

> **JASON:** Seventeen years old, GCSE grade B French, studying Biology, History and Art at College. Available from 1st July–15th August. Has to be home for sister's wedding on August 17th. Likes working with groups of people.
>
> *Because Jason is only seventeen he cannot work for Parents Plus and his availability means he cannot do jobs B or C either. He would be suited to job D because of his interest in art and history plus the fact that he has a good grade in French.*

SHARON: Eighteen years old, has just taken A level French, available until end of September when she starts a secretarial course at college. Likes travel and has been on German and French exchanges from school. Wants to be independent and 'her own boss'.

LLOYD: Eighteen years old, GCSE French Grade D, available from June to end of September. Wants to make money by working for two months and then to travel round.

SUSIE: Seventeen years old, having a year off before going to Cardiff University to study History. Has had work experience previously with a market research organisation. Has studied French and German.

JING: Eighteen years old, speaks English, some Spanish and Chinese. Available from June. She hasn't travelled in Europe before.

2   Choose **one** of the advertised posts and compose your own letter of application. This is a formal letter and should be set out appropriately with your address and the name and address of the person you are writing to included.

In your letter make sure that you describe yourself, say why the position interests you, when you are available and why you think you are suitable for it.

To help you do this, you can invent, and add, details about one extra language you can speak, one skill that you have qualifications in (like typing, cooking or sport) and one piece of relevant experience that will support your application.

3 Write an article for a magazine for young people about summer jobs in Europe for school-leavers and students. The article should be around 350 words long with a lively title and opening paragraph and helpful sub-headings. It will need to mention the kinds of work which are available, the variations in wages and conditions, and the precautions which people should take in applying for work and accepting job offers.

4 Read this letter sent to a travel magazine and published as 'Problem of the Week'. Write your reply, dealing with the points Dorothy Rood makes, as if you worked for the magazine.

> Dear Travel Update,
>
> I'm worried about my daughter, Rachel. She only left school last summer and after a year at college she wants to go off and work somewhere in Germany with one of her friends. She thinks they can work at a holiday camp or something like that.
>
> She wants me to help her with her passport and to sign some papers to say she's eighteen – she will be in three months' time anyway – and I don't know whether I should.
>
> I've heard about young kids just disappearing when they go abroad and being made to carry drugs and things by people they meet and I know Rachel is easily led at times.
>
> I'd be happier with someone keeping an eye on her but I know she's growing up and has to be independent as well. What can I do?
>
> Yours sincerely,
>
>
> Dorothy Rood

MEG 1994

1. SHARON: ~~Thr~~ Sharon would be best suited for Parents Plus. This is because she is eighteen years old which the advert requires you to be. She has A level French which means she will be able to communicate easily with people. Also she wants to be her own boss which this job ables her to be, because the parents will be at work all day.

Lloyd: Would ~~be~~ most suited to a Job at Hotel 'Stromboli'. This is because he will be making money by working. Also the period which he wants to work ~~fits~~ in with when the hotel needs people to work.

Susie: She is a preuniversity student which Marquee Holidays Limited is ~~was~~ looking for, so this is the Job which would suit her best. She has had work experence in market research so she will be use to working with people. She has studied French and will have a vague knowledge of the language. Finally She can work anytime for a whole year so this fits in with the time which the company needs people to work.

Jing: Best suited to Job D ~~because~~ she can speak ~~two~~ languages which the advert requires. Also she is available from June and can work for the minimum of 2 months or she can work longer.

Parents Plus - France
10 Orwell Road
Felixstowe
Suffolk
IP7 7RQ

Craig Scott
3 Park Mount Ave
Baildon
West Yorkshire
England
BD17 6DS

13th March 1997

Dear Sir/Madam,

I am writing in application to the position of a Nanny.

I have just completed a course in A level French which I achieved a grade B. This will able me to communicate adequately with people while over in France.

Also, I have just completed a G.N.V.Q child care course which I also got a top grade in.

The position interests me because it will be the first time in which I am able to combine both my French and my child care.

I am available from the start of May and can work for as long as I am needed.

I have had work experience in a nursery before so I am use to working with children and I am able to look after more than one.

I am looking forward to hear from you at your earliest convenience.

Yours Faithfully
Craig Scott.

Dear Dorothy Road,

I know how hard it is for you to decide whether to let your daughter go to Germany or not. One point which you have got to understand is that in three months' time she will be eighteen, so if she really wants to go she will do with or without your approval. Surely it would be better for you and your daughter if she departs on good terms with you.

It is true that she will be able to work at a German Holiday Camp, as long as she can speak good German,

The only real fear you should have is, as you said the factor of Rachel being made to carry drugs. This is her problem if she is, however if she stay's out of trouble while over in Germany this should not be a problem.

Basically it has got to be her own choice whether to go or not. All you have to do is stand by her in her decision and let her know if she does have any trouble in Germany she can come home without any problems and you will be there for her.

Your Sincerely
Travel Update.

The pages which follow provide advice, in the form of Examiner's tips, on how to tackle the tasks set in this Exam practice section. Read the general points first before turning to the more specific advice given for each particular task.

General Points

On the front of examination papers there is always a certain amount of rubric (advice for you to follow). Always make sure that you read and follow the rubric. Below is a good example:

Pay close attention to what you are asked to write.

PLAN what you are going to write.

Read and check your work before you hand it in.

Any changes to your work should be made clearly.

- Remember that it is a National Curriculum requirement that within any mark scheme there must be separate marks awarded for spelling, handwriting and presentation, so be very attentive to these features of your writing.

- When you are thinking through and preparing your answers do not be afraid to underline and make notes on the examination paper. You may choose to use highlighter pens. What is important is that you think your way through any task before starting to write your answer.

- Make sure that, whatever the task, you include those elements in your writing which distinguish between the pedestrian and the really good – variety of sentence structure including the use of complex sentences, sophisticated vocabulary, perhaps dialogue (correctly punctuated and paragraphed) and so on.

- Look for the number of marks available for a question or task. This is the important sort of clue that you should look for in any examination in any subject. This information will give you a fairly clear idea of the relative difficulty of questions, of the amount of time you should spend on each question and so on.

Task	Examiner's tips

1
- You will probably consider that the teacher is, in fact, very rude, offhand and dismissive. You might even suggest that the teacher is jealous or intimidated which would be a very interesting point. Why do you think the teacher invited the poet in the first place?

- There is also a very solid answer to the second part of the Question 1. The examples are well picked out and the reactions to the points are very sensible, clear and justifiable.

- The third part of Question 1 is rather more difficult. It is right to pick out the references to assonance and rhyme; some of you would have been able to pick up the quotation on Keats and might have had some idea of the sort of poetry written by Kipling. In showing the attitude of the teacher the word "sadly" might well have been picked out also.

- Before launching in to an answer to Question 2 thought should be given both to what you as the poet really thought about the way you were treated and also about who you were speaking to: mother; husband; wife; child etc. Your decisions would then determine your approach to the writing. Quite often there is a second part to an examination paper which asks for a piece of writing with the expectation being at least a side as an answer.

Task	Examiner's tips

2

- There are two tasks here arising from the excerpt from "Motel Chronicles"; the first task is distinctly more straightforward than the second. You are free to choose from the extract any moment which might be considered significant provided that you can give an explanation for your choice. You might, for instance, pick the moment when the boys arrive at the mouth of the tunnel, or the very end of the story when the boy is whipped by his father.

- The second task is rather more difficult and goes right to the heart of "writing from other cultures". You might have a particular and personal perception of American life which you could pursue. Whether or not it is a particularly "correct" or good view is something for you to think about yourself. Certainly you should write carefully about Americanisms in the language and make references to the natural life of the United States. When you are planning an answer for this task it might be an idea to go through the extract marking all the Americanisms and clearly American references. The first reference would be Juvenile Hall; you would pick out words like "creek"; and you would need to understand, "We caught Crawdads with marshmallow bait then tore the shells off them and used their meat to catch more Crawdads"; and so on.

- Key words in the Question 2 are "culture" and "setting" and you should make sure that you deal with both in your answer.

3

- Make sure that you have read all the stimulus material and have used it.

- First of all, this question gives you a context for your writing in that you are asked to provide the text for an information leaflet. If you continue that idea you are then given the ideas for two paragraphs which your text will sensibly contain. There is only a limited space and so you have been given a word length to work to. What you must do therefore is summarise the information.

- Question 2 asks you to reflect on the main article which has been used as stimulus material. You are asked to consider how and why it is interesting and entertaining. You are then pointed to incidents, characters and the writer's use of language. Make sure in your answer you have covered all three of these areas, perhaps especially the writer's use of words.

4

- Whichever one of the tasks you decide on, the same skills are being assessed. The important things to remember are: write in such a way that you can engage and interest the reader; take great care with punctuation – indeed, use punctuation to help you structure your meaning; use paragraphs progressively and wisely; vary your sentence structure so that the style is interesting; check your spellings.

- In terms of the content, don't try to include too much (you are advised to write no more than three sides, which will limit you anyway; candidates who write a lot more tend to ramble!); and remember that not all stories have to be set in the modern world.

- When they see this question, a lot of candidates might think that the first question is bound to be easier (writing about a "dare"), but because the second question is perhaps more challenging, it might encourage better writing.

Task	Examiner's tips

5

- You will have noted that each question is worded in a similar way. In the first part you are asked to provide information – "What happens after the writer leaves the cinema?". In the second part you are asked to give an opinion or to give a justification for what you have just said. The second part of each question is certainly as important as the first; you might even argue that it is more important.

6

- Remember that no one sort of writing is any more worthy than another. If you are given a choice, as you are here, it is a genuine choice. So if you know that you are better writing discursively than you are imaginatively, or vice versa, then choose the type of writing which you prefer.

- Question 1 requires personal writing. A good answer will explore as well as describe a personal experience. For Question 2, the story will need characterisation and settings. Try to avoid stereotypes of characters, and remember there are many possible characters to choose amongst. Question 3 requires a discussion or argument in your writing. You will need to plan your points carefully, perhaps presenting a balanced set of views. The style will probably be more formal.

7

- This is the sort of task which looks very straightforward but which requires a lot of preparation before writing:
  - read the passage carefully and probably several times,
  - analyse carefully the characters and attitudes of the boy and his mother,
  - think carefully about the purpose of the advice you are asked to give and consider the appropriateness of what you want to suggest,
  - there is no indication on the paper – would you be giving the same amount of advice to the mother and the boy or is there more advice you would want to give the one rather than the other?

- This is from a reading paper which means that the majority of the marks are given for demonstrating a clear understanding of what has to be read. This does not, of course, mean that you should not bother about the quality of your writing or presentation but it does mean that you should refer clearly to what you have read.

8

- Make sure that you have read all the material and have used it.
- The questions expect you to write in different and appropriate styles:
  - question 1 expects you to be brief and to the point,
  - question 2 is asking for a formal letter and so you must set it out properly and write in a suitably businesslike style,
  - question 3 is asking you to write for a young people's magazine and so you should use the vocabulary and style which would be right for that sort of publication,
  - question 4 is asking you to write a letter but in the form of those letters you find on a "problem page" in an adult magazine so the style would be chattier and helpful.